FROM THE LIBRARY OF

EXPANDING HORIZONS

EXPANDING

THEOSOPHICAL UNIVERSITY PRESS
PASADENA, CALIFORNIA

JAMES A. LONG

HORIZONS

 A Sunrise Library Book

Library of Congress Catalog Card No. 65-24093
Manufactured in the United States of America

Contents

Introduction

IN EVERY age men and women have pondered on the mystery of existence: where did we come from? why are we here? and what is our ultimate destiny? In our longing to find a philosophy that will prove valid, where can we turn?

If we are sincere in our desire to become an instrument for good in the world, the potency of our aspiration will inevitably lead us to the exact opportunities that will help us attain our goal. Perhaps a book, a magazine or a seemingly chance event — some person or thing will set off a chain-reaction in our consciousness that will draw us, much as iron filings to a magnet, into an entirely new line of thinking and even of circumstance which, if followed through, can change the course of our lives.

Our greatest hope lies in the fact that Truth does exist. Through the millennia it has come down to us like a river whose source is in the Unknown. At times its current flows strong and clear over the surface of the earth, enriching human hearts. At other times, not finding a channel of receptive minds, it disappears and moves quietly underground, and the soil it once made fertile lies fallow. But always the river flows.

How has this "wisdom of the ages" been passed down to us? Has it not been through the lives and works of the great teachers of the past — the Master Jesus, Gautama Buddha, Krishna, Mohammed, Confucius, Lao-tzŭ, Plato and others? Each of them labored with one end in view: to revive in the consciousness of man a recognition of his divine potential and to restate the spiritual values embedded in the sacred traditions of antiquity. Each one, in his own way, helped the river of Truth to flow anew in the fields of human endeavor and to refresh the parched souls of those whose faith had become weakened.

Why do these barren periods recur, when at the core of all the great religions and philosophies we find the identic principles of right thought and action, the selfsame nucleus of inspiration? Was it the fault of the teachers or their teachings? Or was it the inability of their contemporaries to grasp sufficiently the portent of the message and pass it on in its purity? These and many other related questions are considered in the discussions that follow.

But first let us think about some of the preliminary problems that confront us in our search for a larger under-

standing of life's mysteries. To begin with — and this is para-
doxical — neither Christ nor Buddha nor any of those who
taught among men came to establish a world religion. Primitive Christianity, for example, as demonstrated by the life
and influence of Jesus, was a *re*-expression of this ageless
wisdom, but after it was written down and 'explained' by
its myriad exponents, whether in or outside the Church, it
became less and less the universal synthesis of the ethics and
philosophy as given by the Master.

Always it was the disciples and followers of the Christs
and Buddhas who, being deeply stirred by the 'new' revelation, themselves created formal religions and built churches
and temples in the hope of preserving the living message of
their Teacher. As the centuries rolled on, and succeeding
schools of thought imposed *their* interpretations, time and
again the spirit of the original teaching became mired in dead
literalisms. For the very effort to define and credalize automatically restricted the free flow of truth and robbed it of
its power to invigorate and enlighten.

Whatever name or outer form this archaic tradition took
in eras preceding the Christian, in lands to the north or
south, east or west, from the third century A.D. it became
known as *theosophia* — "wisdom of things divine," as taught
in Alexandria by Ammonius Saccas. Concealed from public
knowledge because of the already closing minds of the early
Church Fathers whose theological bickerings are of record,
this wisdom continued as a steady stream of guidance not
alone for the Kabbalists — who studied secretly their "theosophy of the angels" during the dark periods of the Middle
Ages — but acted as stimulus to the leading lights of the
Renaissance: to Paracelsus, Pico della Mirandola, Leonardo

3

da Vinci, Bruno, Kepler and a host of other scientists, philosophers, poets and artists.

Was it an accident that the writings of Jakob Boehme, the "Teutonic theosopher" of the sixteenth century, inspired Saint-Martin in the 1790's to carry on a "theosophic correspondence" with a Swiss philosopher-friend; and that these letters were reprinted in England in 1863 in the hope of reawakening interest in "the theosophic and pure Gospel science involved in these ideas"? And again, that Emerson and others, stimulated by the cosmic insights of the *Bhagavad-Gītā*, spearheaded the Transcendentalist movement in America in the 1830's?

According to tradition, the great Tibetan reformer Tsong-Kha-pa (1357?-1419) prophesied that during the final quarter of each century thereafter a marked spiritual impetus would be felt, particularly in the West. While this revitalizing current in the immediately succeeding centuries is not easy to identify, it seems to have found expression in certain illuminated individuals as well as within the secret chambers of the Fire-Philosophers, Alchemists and Kabbalists. In the eighteenth and nineteenth centuries the impulse becomes more clearly traceable — not that a new religion was founded, but seeds were sown in the soil of the centuries-to-be that were later to flower into an expanded moral outlook.

Toward the end of the eighteenth century, coincident with the American and French Revolutions, the first major crack in the religious isolationism which had dominated Europe occurred with the breakthrough into Western intellectual circles of the rich philosophic content of Oriental literature. But it was not until the closing decades of the nineteenth century that the vivifying force, reaching every corner of the thinking world, gained sufficient momentum to carry over into our present century.

This impetus was climaxed by the publication of *The Secret Doctrine* by H. P. Blavatsky in 1888, her comprehensive examination of the world's (not only Christian) sacred literatures revealing that the key thoughts in all of them were as jewels strung on one golden thread: man's divine origin and destiny. By no means unimportant was the reintroduction into Occidental thought of the once universally accepted doctrine of reincarnation — the periodic return of the soul to earth experience. Thus the ancient river which had been so long buried under the silt of dogmatic accretions once more flowed above ground.

All human progress has sprung from the repeated effort of the soul of man to give expression to those primeval spiritual ideas that were implanted deep within the memory of the race when it first found its home upon this globe. In the long course of our pilgrimage, we have moved from unselfconsciousness to an awareness of ourselves, and finally to a recognition of our individual moral responsibility — a responsibility which has undergone many and varied transformations.

Evolution from the material standpoint has been rapidly approaching a cyclic zenith, but now there is a new evolutionary impulse trying to manifest which will have to come to light through the very medium that is tending to hold it back. It is to the strength of the divine seed growing within the hard shell of materiality, to the surge of spiritual and moral force in the relationships of men, that we turn our eyes in these critical days.

We have indeed reached a turning point, beyond which

we dare no longer submit to the rigidity of dogma. The increasing number of laymen who are reading the world's religious and philosophic classics are refusing to accept any one faith as the final word of truth or the only avenue of salvation. Colleges and universities likewise are encouraging a more universal approach and, in an effort to discover the unifying thread of wisdom, are offering regular courses in comparative religions.

Just as the physical sun reveals different phases of solar activity, depending upon which of the various wave lengths is used to photograph it, so every one of the sacred scriptures contains several levels of inspiration. We may read the parables and legends that surround a teacher as a historic account of his birth, accomplishments and teaching; or, using another wave length, we may see him as a Savior, flashing across the horizon of human experience as a solar god, to leave a light and a hope for millennia; or, still again, we may in the simple practice of his precepts find courage for daily living.

It should be obvious, then, that this wisdom-religion comprises the most profound reaches of knowledge as well as the purest ethics. The keystone thought in the arch is that at the heart of all is divinity — within, without, above, below — divinity seeking expression that it might illumine the environment into which its influence is born. The tragedy is that for many, many centuries we have been wont to consider, not by choice but by miseducation, that we are worms of the dust. We have not been taught that as potential gods we must rediscover for ourselves the ways and means to become, in time, self-conscious co-workers with nature. It is a beautiful and strengthening vision, for through the delicate and just balancing of cause and effect the cycles of activity and rest in turn allow for the ever-unfolding growth of the godlike qualities within each one of us.

But we shall find ourselves marooned in the shallows if we become involved solely in the intricacies of technical doctrine. We can be assured that the Protectors of the race would not have taken so great pains to preserve in seed form — in myth, legend, symbol and stone — a knowledge of these traditions merely to fascinate the intellect. This wisdom has been reiterated from age to age, because behind every phase of teaching is an ethical concept that must be recognized and exemplified. The whole effort springs from a compassionate urge to give us fresh hope and to keep alive man's flaming intuition.

Truth, like happiness, cannot be bought. It must be earned, and the more sincere we are the more alert must we be to distinguish the genuine from the counterfeit. The difference is not always apparent, for not every activity calling itself religious or metaphysical is built upon a selfless spiritual foundation. Since the restatement of the ancient and universal philosophy by H. P. Blavatsky, the West especially has been deluged with numerous minor prophets who, pursuing one or more half-truths, have erected thereon glittering structures of fantasy. It is not our purpose to judge of their merit or demerit. Time will separate the wheat from the chaff.

But let it be thoroughly understood that we have no interest in nor can we condone any of the pseudo-spiritual practices rampant today: psychism, phenomena-hunting, development of the so-called occult powers, hatha-yoga exercises, initiations into special mysteries — in most cases for a price. However disguised, all of these are nothing more than appeals to the selfishness in human nature. Those of us who

7

have had our fingers burned by one or another of these pseudoisms have learned, after much pain and difficulty, that the pathway to truth is indeed "strait and narrow," but it is the only path that will lead us surely to our goal.

It has been my privilege over the years to "think out loud" with individuals and groups of people in various parts of the world. As I talked with them, one thing stood out above all else — their search for a workable philosophy to which they could inwardly anchor and the corresponding need to confirm their intuitive feeling that there *is* an explanation of the many paradoxes and problems of life. Recognizing that civilization but reflects the growth and development of human character, our discussions explored those spiritual principles which can be applied to any situation, regardless of one's creed, politics, education or social background. For whatever roadway of experience anyone may travel, there is always a common ground of values on which to meet.

Much of the material in this volume, representing the fruit of an exchange of ideas with hundreds of men and women, has appeared in *Sunrise* magazine and, while considerable editing has been done, we have tried to retain the informality of the original discussions. Should anyone, however, be looking for a cut and dried formula of instruction that will bring him enlightenment, he will be disappointed. Each one of us is unique, an individual expression of his own inner self, and hence in the final analysis must search out and follow that pathway of endeavor that is his and his alone.

There is no stock answer that will cover the need of all — no book, no teacher, no source outside of man himself — for who can tell another what he requires for growth? The one guide and mentor is *Life*. Once an individual through the natural processes of his awakening consciousness finds the touchstone of truth within himself, he will know that its authority stems not from this or that person whose writings he may have read or whose conversations he may have enjoyed, but arises from the depths of his own soul.

— J.A.L.

The Moving Finger writes; and, having writ,
Moves on: nor all thy Piety nor Wit
    Shall lure it back to cancel half a Line,
Nor all thy Tears wash out a Word of it.
        — *Rubáiyát* of OMAR KHAYYÁM

Script of Destiny

IF WE BELIEVE that the law of Order and Harmony that prevails in celestial spheres is reflected in the world of human affairs, then we must know that what a man sows in the field of his character he will reap accordingly, whether in this life, or in some future arena of experience. And if we seriously consider our lives from this perspective, we realize that every circumstance in which we find ourselves today *we*

11

must have created somewhere along the line. That being the case, surely there is not a moment that is without purpose, for are we not in very truth on a ladder of evolution, midway between the atoms and the stars — with each and all evolving and growing and learning to bring forth their own measure of godhood?

The mills of the gods grind slowly, yet they grind exceedingly small. What we sow, we must reap — the Eastern writings call this *karma*, implying that every action is followed by its corresponding reaction. It is a useful word, now adopted into the English language, because it comprehends the whole philosophy of harmony and justice as well as the compassionate provision of nature that allows a man to learn with exceeding thoroughness by meeting the results of his thinking and deeds.

So let us watch the daily unfolding of events in the light of the promptings from within and without, and we may perceive through the maze of action and reaction, of sowing and reaping, of giving and receiving on the objective plane, an "Ariadne" thread of guidance. If the works of the Divine are manifest through all things, then there is not a person we meet or an event that occurs but represents an opportunity for growth and a positive guide in the conduct of our lives. The same law that burns us when we touch the flame operates on the moral and spiritual planes as well, and it will continue to bring pain and sorrow of one kind or another until we awake to the fact that our better self is trying, desperately at times, to tell us something. And as we observe what is transpiring within our souls, we shall recognize that the quality or focus of our concern is gradually being raised from a lower to a higher level of consciousness.

We all have different ideas as to why there is suffering, but nature knows no more beneficent way to alert us to our limitations or to the wrongs we do than by permitting us to meet the precise effects of our foolish and selfish acts — just as we benefit to the last jot and tittle by the results of every truly unselfish thought and deed. This whole process of adjustment accents the selfless facet of nature, which acts and reacts as impersonally as the sun and the rain.

It is the immortal element in us that is the source of our greatest inspiration and strength, for it carries within itself the wisdom and knowledge of all our past, the indestructible record of our suffering and aspiration, our hopes and our dreams. It is the recorder of all things thought and done, from which flow the effects of causes set in motion today, yesterday, and in lives gone by.

Thus in the cosmic book of destiny, there is no recording angel to allot divine reward or satanic punishment. It is man alone who has inscribed his past, who must read and interpret his present, and in so doing shape his future. We cannot hope to decipher the entire script of our lives at once, but we should try to read the signposts of direction as they come. Our main drawback is in expecting karma to work too fast or according to our wishes. But as we understand more clearly our own particular chapter in the larger, universal script of destiny, we shall observe that the circumstances and events that arise day by day operate so scientifically, so accurately, and so compassionately that all whom we contact are of necessity brought to us and we to them for each of us to learn and to grow, to receive and to give. It is a natural and beautiful interchange of experience and, if we can quietly 'feel' the karma as it unfolds from moment to moment, we shall begin to recognize the promptings of guidance. If, however, we anxiously hunt for signposts, we shall never see them. That is the paradox: when we seek for this or that specific form of help, it never comes; but if we meet each day unafraid, relying on our innate strength and wisdom, we shall have all the protection and help we can use.

Let us not delude ourselves, however, and fancy that real knowledge or inspiration will come to us if we just passively sit down and wait. All growth in understanding is achieved by consciously fulfilling our whole duty in every area of our responsibility. If we can keep this ideal in the background of our consciousness, we will instinctively look beneath the outer events and penetrate to the principle and essence behind them. When we do that, the inner value, the spirit and not merely the letter, of each experience becomes a part of our character, and life takes on a new atmosphere.

If we have had many lives in the past, surely we shall have repeated sojourns on earth in the future; some may be pleasant and successful by outer standards, others a veritable nightmare of frustration and trial. The author of our life, who is none other than ourself, has so designed the lights and shades of our present experience that we, with our free will and whatever intelligence and purity of aspiration we can muster, may perceive what qualities in our characters need reshaping, and what pillars of strength we may build on. Our greatest mistake lies in trying to get through the difficult periods as quickly as possible, forgetting entirely that the hellish moments are preparing us to give birth to something of immeasurable value which otherwise might be stillborn. How few of us when our happier moments arrive think of sharing with our fellowmen the golden values that are found in the crucible of suffering? As soon as better times appear, we avidly enjoy them, unmindful of the beauty and enrichment that accompanied the pain. That is why easy experiences can represent our most dangerous periods; difficult ones the most fruitful.

Thanks to the creative essence behind the universe, every minute particle in the cosmos is bipolar. Hence the most negative situation can be turned into a positive one, and the most material condition can be viewed from the spiritual pole of experience. We gain great strength from the over-coming of difficulties; even the minor stumbling blocks have merit, if we welcome all circumstances as part of our treasury of opportunity. The hurdles and obstacles that arise in the line of natural duty are the result of the long-term discipli-nary responsibility of our higher self — for the progress of the individual, and indeed of the whole of humankind, is built upon self-conquest.

Thus there is not a thing that happens but carries with it an opportunity to adjust our attitudes and consciousness toward a larger vision and a more understanding feeling for others. If it is a problem, we are challenged to meet and solve it; if a sorrow, to try to feel the compassionate work-ing of the Law through it all; and if a joy, to see how and where we might share its blessing. Nevertheless, I do not believe that every trial or difficulty is the effect of wrong-doing. Error and weakness do bring suffering in their wake, obviously, for that is nature's surest way of teaching. But there is a higher karma that may draw us magnetically into the valleys of pain in order to shock us out of our old and comfortable grooves into fresh pathways of thought.

We touch here the inner aspect of the unfolding script

of our lives: when any individual sincerely strives to expand his consciousness, to become an impersonal servant of his spiritual will, he begins to activate the Christos-element within him. When that occurs, his consciousness shines a little brighter, and his higher self or guardian angel, recognizing the intensity of the call, dare not neglect it. Nature then provides that which is needed for him to prove the strength and fidelity of his aspiration. The Law operates in spite of your or my weakness or strength, and what a man *is* in the deepest recesses of his soul will be seen. No set rules or regulations, no Bible or Vedas or any sacred text alone, will help him now. He can know all the technical facets of the structure of atoms and galaxies, all about the many principles in the human constitution, but unless he has fulfilled the requirements of duty in every aspect of his nature, he cannot open the gate to wisdom. This path of growth may seem a lonely one, but it is a path of joy. Once we put the high principles of right thought into our every action, we shall know that the divinity that enlivens both atom and star also enfolds man.

Absolute trust in the Law brings into being an inner force that follows the lines of least resistance and circulates through the body of humanity. For the purity of one's devotion and loyalty will function without regard to time or place, to do the right good that you and I could not conceive of or predict or control. We do not need to know how it works; but if nature is endeavoring to allow divinity to reflect itself in every portion of the universe we can feel assured that, wherever enlightened hearts beat, good will follow and lessen by so much the burden of ugliness and evil in the world.

The Moving Finger writes — if we will try to read the script of our lives in this atmosphere of thought, we may find ourselves, unconsciously, becoming natural agents of protection to our fellowmen in the scheme of divine guardianship that is built around humanity.

Karma: Law of Cause and Effect

QUESTION — I would like to know more about karma, particularly with regard to the idea that we are responsible for our circumstances in life. Could we discuss this a little?

Comment — This is a subject that never loses interest. You will remember how the New Testament expresses the thought: "whatsoever a man soweth, that shall he also reap." That is just what *karma* means — it is a Sanskrit term used in Hindu and Buddhist philosophy to signify 'action' followed by reaction. Every religion has stressed the doctrine of moral responsibility. The Moslems speak of Kismet as representing one's individual portion or lot in life. The ancient Greeks had their Nemesis or goddess of retributive justice; they also personified past, present and future as the three Moirai or Spinners of Destiny. So too those born in the Jewish faith are familiar with the Mosaic injunction: "an eye for an eye, and a tooth for a tooth." All of these are different ways of describing the universal law of harmony and balance, which insures that every cause set in motion will, some time in the future, bring about its corresponding effect.

What first appeals to one in the study of karma is the potency of thought it stirs in us when we think of it in connection with its companion doctrine of rebirth, and the part that each of us has to play in the long drama of existence. The tendency to guard against is that of narrowing our thinking down to 'me and my karma'; we can become so involved in our personal concerns that we fail to view our day to day experiences practically and intelligently in the light of the larger picture.

There are many aspects of karma, such as world, national and racial karma, family as well as individual karma. We can even say there is business karma, community karma, and so forth. In other words, in every avenue of experience, from the individual to the international, men are thinking and acting and hence setting certain causes in motion which are bound to have their effects. So there is no end to the ramifications of actions and reactions.

Question — Just how did all this begin?

Comment — To get a truer perspective of karma in relation to the present, we have to go way back, to the time of the Garden of Eden. We have been told that from the day when man tasted of the fruit of the tree of knowledge of good and evil he became a self-conscious unit of the human kingdom, ethically responsible for his every thought and act. If this is so, then from that point on we have been the shapers of our character and the makers of our destiny; and that divine law of sowing and reaping has allowed us to create the very circumstances in which we find ourselves today — whatever their quality.

It is regrettable, however, that we in the West have been trained to think of the operation of this law with fear in our hearts: "if you don't live right, God will punish you; if you do wrong, you won't go to heaven." It is difficult to conceive of any God watching each individual, ready to strike him down if he errs; or if he is good, to reward him with specially contrived favors. Man may have been "fearfully and wonderfully made," but it does not follow that he was made in fear. The curse of dogmatic belief that we were born in sin has had effects both far-reaching and devastating. Man *is* wonderfully made, and with the qualities of the highest potential in his nature — qualities founded on a divine trust and not a divine fear. The Almighty Intelligence which pervades every minute atom of our universe could not have allowed its essence to manifest without a complete trust that each such atom in time would become as that from which it sprang. To limit our concepts to a Deity who would on the one hand personally supervise this whole evolutionary unfoldment, individual by individual, and on the other hand relegate us to 'sin' at birth, is to degrade the true purpose of life.

There is a vast amount of hidden truth involved in the allegory of the Fallen Angel. This story, so poorly conceived in the orthodox interpretation, is told by many ancient peoples. In the Hindu tradition it is symbolized by the descent of *Mānasaputras* or "Sons of Mind" — godlike beings who lighted the fires of the human mind, much as in Greek mythology Prometheus brought the "fire" of the gods to men. So in the Bible, the casting out of Adam and Eve from Paradise signified humanity's transition from a childlike phase of growth into a state of conscious individual responsibility.

When we realize that you and I from that moment in our evolutionary cycle have been on our own, we begin to get a fuller picture of what this doctrine of karma implies. It means that we, being novices in the use of our free will, made many, many blunders. And every time we made a mistake we felt a reaction to it, attempting to point our thought in the direction of not falling into the same error again. We all learn soon enough on the physical plane, but it takes us much longer to learn lessons on the moral and spiritual levels. Nevertheless, nature's law of harmony operates always to restore equilibrium, sometimes in quite a potent manner, but it is in this way that gradually we attain discrimination.

It boils down to the simple fact that through the ages we have accumulated a lot of effects of former actions so that we are faced now with a collection of karmic responsibilities dating from the far past, from which the immortal element in us has chosen a certain portion for this lifetime. This portion is neither too heavy nor too light, as perfect justice rules throughout the entire cosmos.

People sometimes speak of good karma and bad karma, pleasant and unpleasant. To me there is no such thing as good or bad karma, for the results, the effects of our actions and thoughts, are nothing more nor less than opportunity. That is the key. Karma as opportunity gives everybody the same possibility of growth. Now I don't consider that a heavy load to bear. All we need do is temper our reactions to our circumstances and meet them with the right attitude. But if we are foolish enough to feel revulsion to the so-called unpleasant events of life, we extend the effects of wrong causes further and further until finally we wake up and realize that we are rebelling against nothing but ourselves.

It makes no difference how much suffering we may have in this lifetime — our karma will never be more than we can handle. Point out an individual with a heavy karmic load, and you will have pointed out a strong soul. The man who is going through real torment is a soul who has earned, by the strength of his inner aspiration, the right to test the metal of himself to the core.

Question — If we knew what we had done in the past that had brought on our present problems, wouldn't it be easier to understand them? I know I am responsible for whatever comes to me, both the pleasant and unpleasant things. But how can I handle all of this karma in the right way?

Comment — If nature in its highest sense is harmonious and kind and just, it seems to me it would not ask us to meet a responsibility without providing a key or a guide, and especially would this be true with one who is consciously aspiring. Nature does provide that key, though we are having a hard time finding it. But if we believe there cannot be a cause without an effect, or an effect without a cause, we must believe that nothing happens by chance. Every situation we are confronted with, then, is the result of something we thought or did or participated in in the past that has attracted to us the effects represented by the circumstances

23

in which we now find ourselves. Do we need to know the exact cause? We cannot know it in detail, but we can and should try to discern the *quality* of experience that brought about our present situation.

At this stage of our growth, those who are actively trying to improve their character, to self-direct their own evolution, are beginning to sense the first faint glimmerings of a genuine intuition. We are not anywhere near the flowering of our present racial cycle, but we are at the same time being called upon to handle the early pushings of the seed of intuition in our consciousness. Therefore, when anyone begins to think about the doctrines of karma and reincarnation he is compelled, sooner or later, to recognize that he has a definite responsibility to meet intelligently the karma that is his. He will have to learn *how* to meet it, how to listen to the imploring of his immortal self, his intuition, if you please. It is the immortal self that has selected the drama of this incarnation in which he is the actor, and it is this higher element that is endeavoring by and through the circumstances of life to guide him to meet with a proper attitude the challenges of each day.

Thus in our struggles toward a fuller understanding, we begin to realize we can develop the ability to read the unfolding karmic script of our lives. When we work with this, then we find ourselves better able to feel out the situations as they arise, and deal with them more intelligently. We can think of it as a Book — the Book of records as the Koran calls it — in which is inscribed in its entirety our individual life. Each of our days, representing a page of so-called karmic merit and demerit, will contain the signposts, the impellings and repellings, the conscience knocks, and even the intuitions that are there to be utilized. Once we are able even slightly to read the daily script of our experiences, we realize something else: that there is a direct relation between the quality of a reaction and the quality of action that brought it into being. This is not going to be spelled out, but if we keep in mind that our major task in the long run is to unfold fully the divine values within us, we will know that the process of transmuting the lower by the higher self must be accompanied by a continued effort to improve the quality of our attitude in every circumstance.

Question — In trying to improve our attitude toward our own karma, shouldn't we also take into account the karma of those around us? I am thinking especially of family and national karma.

Comment — If we believe in the natural working of this law, then those we meet each day we meet by karma, and either we receive something from them or they receive something from us, as the result of that contact. Neither party may be aware of any conscious exchange. It happens as simply as breathing, and may have only an infinitesimal effect, but all of it together helps make up the karmic balance, the karmic total of the day. When we maintain the best inner attitude we can, keeping our personal will as the servant, allowing the spiritual will or the intuition to have as free rein as possible, we begin to recognize what the other person has contributed toward the expansive elements available to us at any time.

Question — But isn't it presumptuous to assume that we could deliberately have any effect on the karma of nations?

We are doing very well, aren't we, if we can deal intelligently with our personal lives?

Comment — Most of us cannot directly do anything about national or world karma. Nevertheless, we are part of humanity, and as we strengthen our character, so will our nation and the world at large benefit. The basic key is duty: we fulfill our destiny best by doing the duties that lie immediately before us. Should it happen that you or I by natural karma find ourselves a member of Congress or Parliament, then we would have the opportunity to contribute more potently and directly to our respective countries. What matters most is where we are today and what we are doing about it, for it is the quality of our thoughts and actions that will condition our influence in the future.

Don't you see what a marvelous opportunity we have? Reacting creatively and with a will to correct past errors, we will inevitably impress upon the consciousness of our fellowmen the quality of our endeavor and by so much give them added courage. Without fear but with full trust we can move forward from where we are, knowing that our right thoughts and right actions will in time have their due effects. It makes each moment an opportunity — a challenging opportunity to fulfill our destined responsibilities, not alone to ourselves but to all mankind.

The Lord's Prayer

QUESTION — If we get what we earn, and are rewarded or penalized for our actions, then just what can we expect from prayer?

Comment — This subject is an important one and has many implications. But before we can begin to discuss the matter of prayer, it is advisable to drop from our consciousness the idea of an anthropomorphic Personal God enthroned in space, who dispenses good or evil, either according to His whim or fancy, or according to our desires. That concept, I feel, is erroneous; it denies justice and undermines faith — faith in the ultimate harmony of universal law.

Actually, the practical essence of prayer, as the Master Jesus conceived it, is contained in his Gethsemane supplication: "Not my will, but Thine be done" — not my personal desire, but the will of the Divine. In other words, let the law of justice work its harmonizing and balancing effect, so that causes previously set in motion may work themselves out in our lives.

Question — If we with our personal wills seek special help now and get it, even if we know we don't really deserve it, would we be extending our credit, and must we pay in equivalent coin later?

Comment — While intense prayer of the personal-will type might temporarily divert the effects of specific causes, and in that sense only could we say that our "credit is extended," we can be mighty sure that the exact effect of every cause will, *in time*, catch up with us — and often with interest compounded. For let us not imagine that any amount of prayer will nullify the action of the great law of balance. There is no 'remission of sin' in the sense commonly understood. Neither prayer nor 'forgiveness' can alter the inflexibility of nature's universal working, and effect will follow cause, no matter how great a span of time may intervene between the one and the other.

Question — Probably everyone prays in one way or another, and of course we know that Jesus did — at least he is credited with the Lord's Prayer. Now there are parts of that prayer that don't seem to add up, yet I have heard it said that one can find the whole philosophy of life in it.

28

Comment — The Lord's Prayer does contain a whole philosophy of *living*. But prayer as it is generally practiced has wandered far from the injunctions of the Master Jesus and indeed of all the great world teachers. Prayer today takes a variety of forms, nearly all of which may be classed as selfish: at best, they center on the needs of oneself rather than on others; and at the worst, they are nothing more nor less than an exploitation of one's divine heritage. By this I refer to those techniques of prayer that are becoming increasingly popular, whereby so-called "power, wealth and intellectual vigor" may be had by concentrating on what *we* want. This type of prayer is packed with concentrated selfishness, and as such is extremely dangerous to the spiritual progress of the individual who practices it.

When fully understood, there is not one iota of selfishness in the Lord's Prayer. And yet who of us really grasps what the Master meant? We learn the prayer in childhood; in adulthood we hear it recited with variations of piety; while in hymn it is sung by choirs the world over. But how has it affected our day to day thinking?

Question — I imagine we've all gone through a number of stages in our thinking about prayer. We all learned the common forms of prayer in church and Sunday school, but these never appealed to me as being practical. Nor did they seem what prayer should accomplish, in that most of this praying was with the idea of doing something to or for myself. Somehow I never felt that I had the right to ask for anything, having had so much in comparison with others. I rather felt like giving thanks for what I had, instead of asking for more, and thus attempting in some way to pay the freight, so to say, on my stay here. I never could see the idea of praying to any being, nor to any Deity directly, for the accomplishment of any specific earthly purpose. But I have always felt that just as in the field of physics nature runs things according to law, so it must be in spiritual things: you will receive in direct proportion to that which you give. What then is the benefit you receive from praying?

Question — I also have never felt I had the right to ask for things. Praying has always meant to me just *asking;* and while I didn't have any Personal God I could recognize, or any anthropomorphic Being to ask favors of, just so I couldn't find anybody in particular to thank.

Comment — I understand exactly what you mean. There is a world of difference between the concept of a God somewhere off in space outside of man, who is supposed to be directly responsible for all that happens after he created us, and the idea of a Divine Intelligence at the heart of everything within the universe, from atom to sun to each of us. If we have this latter concept, then when it comes to praying we find ourselves thinking of the Lord's Prayer no longer as a means of having our petitions answered, but rather as a verbal expression of the highest aspiration man is capable of feeling.

Our Father which art in heaven, Hallowed be thy name — Here the Master addresses himself to the Father within, which is not fully incarnated in us because we haven't yet reached that point where we have become one with it. Keeping in mind St. Paul's division of man into body, soul and spirit, we may consider the Father within each one of us as an aspect of that Divine Intelligence, which it is our supreme responsibility to become like unto. This will take long eons of time, but man has the potential because of that spark of the Divine manifesting in every living organism.

Thy kingdom come — Here we ask that the kingdom of the Father, which resides in heaven or the spiritual realms, and also within, should come into being. That is, we pray or aspire for the ability to bring into active manifestation right here on earth that Divine aspect of our nature, without which we would not exist.

Thy will be done in earth, as it is in heaven — Let the works of the Divine Intelligence find their way into all the affairs of life on this earth, as they have found expression in heaven — heaven being the relatively ideal as well as the potential quality that we one day will develop.

Give us this day our daily bread — Note, *this day*, our *daily* bread. We are not enjoined to secure the needs for all of futurity; nor does "our daily bread" signify merely the physical needs, important as these are. Give us *this day* whatever is required in the way of strength, vision and wisdom, not only for ourselves but for our family, neighbor, community, perhaps our nation, and all mankind. Those needs may run the gamut from the most ordinary to the highest qualities of character that we are in the process of developing and thus making pliable to the Father within.

And forgive us our debts, as we forgive our debtors — Here is one of the most practical rules of esoteric training, and yet one of the most misunderstood. This prayer does not ask the Father to forgive us our transgressions in the sense of absolving us from the responsibility to correct them. Nor are we to pray for forgiveness or to ask for ourselves qualities of character that we in turn have not expressed in our relations with others. Just as we do not hold against our brothers their mistakes, so we ask the Father within, whose compassion is greater than ours, not to hold against us the errors in judgment we are making in our struggle to evolve. The old law of balance, of harmony, is operating here, the law of karma. *As ye sow, that shall ye reap* — action followed by its corresponding reaction holds good unto eternity. Just as karma is one side of the coin, so compassion or mercy is the other side of the same universal law. But we must remove from our hearts all rancor or resentment against injustices done to *us* before "praying for mercy" to the Father within as regards the injustices we daily commit against our real Self.

And lead us not into temptation, but deliver us from evil — Taken literally this is an extraordinary statement. If this prayer is addressed to God, supposedly the father of all good, what an insult to ask him not to lead us into temptation. Or is there a more inspiring interpretation? "O Father within, lead us not *away* from our trials and difficulties, so that meeting them squarely we may recognize evil for what it is and overcome its power to control."

Question — I like that far better. I never could understand why we had to beg the Father not to lead us into evil ways, and I've always wondered why this was included in a prayer supposed to have been given by a Savior.

Comment — You're not the only one who has puzzled over this. Probably every thinking person has tried to figure out some interpretation that could satisfy his innate sense of ethics. In fact, some years ago an Episcopal clergyman urged that the Lord's Prayer be revised. He suggested that the phrase be changed to read: "And let us not fall when tempted," because, as he explained, "no Christian can expect to be spared temptation," and therefore the prayer should petition for "the strength to resist temptation."

Certainly that attitude, rather than the weak supplication to be spared every enticement, arouses our manhood. Who is the stronger, the more compassionate, the wiser, in the final analysis: the man who has been shielded from all the distractions of life, or he who having been challenged by temptations has recognized them for what they were and battled his way out to land on his feet? Assuredly the latter, for that man can be counted on; he has strengthened the inner fiber of his soul.

For thine is the kingdom, and the power, and the glory, for ever. I understand that some authorities consider this phrase to be a later addition. Whatever the case, we can interpret it in this way — the Divine Intelligence is the real kingdom and the only real power, and when its works are made manifest on this earth, in the lives of each one of us, then truly is it seen as a glory for ever and ever.

What then does the Lord's Prayer add up to in relation to karma? We find that nature's inviolable law of cause and effect is working toward one end: the restoration of balance and harmony. Man therefore has the responsibility to work consciously toward that goal. In so doing, we discover that prayer becomes the performance of duty in the light of our daily responsibility to our guardian angel who watches over every aspect of our lives. To the degree that we cooperate with that divine Inspirer will we become an expression, not of our personal wills, but of the spiritual will of the Father within.

Beyond Death — New Life

QUESTION — In our discussions the idea of rebirth has come up. At first I thought it fantastic that after I died I would come back again. But the more I toss it around and the more my brain works out all sorts of arguments against it, the more I feel there is something to it. When and how did this idea of reincarnation get started?

Comment — I could no more tell you when reincarnation got started than I could tell you when the sun and the moon and the stars began their orderly and harmonious courses. All I can say is that the principle of ebb and flux appears to be one of nature's "eternal ways," for the law of cyclic progression is as old as the world. It was in process when the solar system came into being; and again, still farther removed in space and time, it was a habit when our home-universe, with its numberless galaxies and solar systems, first burst forth from the darkness of Space. On our earth its expressions are manifold: day and night, light and darkness, activity and rest — all different and individual modes of the ebb and flux of life in movement. Everything in nature is thus subject to this one law of renewal of form, birth and death, death and birth, in order to provide fresh vehicles for the indwelling spirit. Reincarnation refers to the rebirth of the soul here on earth — a specific application of the general law of renewal or reimbodiment.

Question — But the idea of reincarnation is new to so many of us. Of course I remember from my college days that Shelley, Wordsworth and Tennyson, and Goethe too, spoke of other worlds from which they had come, and that they "had been here before." I thought it mere poetic fancy. I loved the beauty of their creations, but it never occurred to me they might really mean it literally. As I get older, I'm not so certain. Was this belief known in other ages?

Comment — It was indeed; in fact, if we peruse the writings of the Orient, of Asia Minor and of Greece and Persia, we find clear indications of a belief, in one form or another, in the idea of rebirth. For sacred tradition maintains that you and I are truly gods in essence, potential divinities, in ceaseless activity, striving to find our way; and in that striving, whether we are conscious of it or not, we, as human beings, have been moving in and out of this earth for countless ages, because the basic habit of nature is to evolve in spiral fashion

— action followed by reaction, cause by effect. Therefore the idea of rebirth was always linked up with the concept of justice: that what a man sows now, he will have to reap later as the round of the cycle of cause and effect turns on itself, whether in this life or some future existence. However, let me warn you that there are many wrong ideas in regard to reincarnation.

For example, some of the Eastern beliefs lead one to suppose that if you live an evil life you may return as an animal. But that is because their presentations have become in certain respects as dogmatic as ours. I do not believe the *original* Hindu and Buddhist doctrine implied the transmigration of the *soul* into animal bodies after death, though in their texts you will find passages that seem to uphold this view. But these have reference merely to the temporary transmigration of certain of the lower elements of 'the man that was' into the bodies of the lower kingdoms. As said, this has nothing whatever to do with the reincarnating *soul*.

Question — You mean there's no chance of our returning as an animal, even by mistake?

Comment — No chance whatever, for it would be absolutely contrary to nature's forward moving processes for the human soul to retrograde into a vehicle less than human. That is *not* reincarnation or reimbodiment as the sages of every land and of all ages have taught it, but is a degenerated belief which is false, utterly out of harmony with the facts.

The true and original doctrine of rebirth or reincarnation emphasizes this one point: "Once a man, always a man" — until you become something greater. Think for a moment of the enormous injustice to the soul of man if, by some feat of dark magic, it were forced to incarnate in the body of an animal, with no outlet of expression for the divine-human qualities. Just try to imagine yourself, with your degree of self-consciousness and intelligence, looking at a glorious sunset out of the eyes of your pet dog, and feel the torture and the agony of imprisonment that experience would be.

No! Once we with the help of our divine spark have earned *human* expression, we will not retrogress; unless — and this is the one exception — by willful evil-doing over a long series of lives the soul deliberately breaks the link with its Father within. Then, in its self-determined retrogression, it becomes truly a "lost" soul — having lost its right to participate in the forward evolutionary current. Fortunately, such a "break" from divine contact is rare indeed; if it does occur, then the individual atomic elements formerly governed by the "lost" soul, because of being so impregnated with subhuman tendencies, may find outlet in forms of life lower than the human, in animal and even in plant vehicles. *But this is not the destiny of the aspiring human soul* which, linked with its divinity, is seeking expansion of understanding and consciousness with each new rebirth on earth.

Question — That's quite a picture. But why aren't we taught about reincarnation in church?

Comment — That's a long story, and I wouldn't attempt to give the reason why the early Church Fathers in handling the texts of the Christian Scriptures either eliminated or at least excluded certain relevant teachings which touched not only on the concept of rebirth, but on other matters dealing with the soul's relation to the whole solar system. These ideas would have provided a much broader and more universal philosophy than is now contained in the Creed. In fact, the very teaching of the soul's need for repetitive experiences on earth was publicly anathematized in one of the early Church Councils. In other words, it was formally stricken from the *required* belief of the Christian Church — an event which marked one of the stages in the crystallization and hence the decline of the true Christianity. For once the message of the Master Jesus no longer represented to the peoples of the day *a vital and growing search for truth*, but had settled down into a well-defined and organized belief, then the Creed of the Church rather than man's own inner guide became his monitor. Yet, even in the Scriptures as they are today, you can find references to the idea of rebirth. You have to dig for them, because they are casual rather than direct; nevertheless they point to the then popular acceptance of rebirth by the peoples of Asia Minor.

Question — Where can we find such references in the Bible?

Comment — The first one that comes to mind is in *Matthew*, I believe, where Jesus asked his disciples: "Whom do men say that I the Son of man am?" And they replied: "Some say that thou art John the Baptist: some, Elias; and others, Jeremias, or one of the prophets." Now why would Jesus have tossed a question like that to his disciples, unless the idea of rebirth was commonly accepted? He didn't ask whether or not people thought he might have lived before, but taking that for granted he asked simply *who* they thought he might have been.

And what about the story of the blind man in the *Gospel of St. John?* We all know it, where Jesus passed by a man blind *from birth,* and his disciples asked him: "Master, who did sin, this man, or his parents, that he was born blind?" And do you remember Jesus' answer? — "Neither hath this man sinned, nor his parents: but that the works of God should be made manifest in him." Note again that Jesus did not bother to expatiate on whether the man had or had not lived before — the question asked by the disciples takes that for granted, for the man could not have sinned in this life if he was blind from birth. The significant point here is that Jesus lifts the whole concept of action and reaction, cause and effect, from a mere "eye for an eye" atmosphere into the larger, the more compassionate view, that karma is not punitive, not necessarily a retributive experience, but always *the soul's opportunity for growth.* Thus he showed the blindness not as a punishment, but as an avenue of experience whereby the "works of God [one's inner god] might be made manifest"; whereby the Law, or the working out of the blind man's inherent destiny, might be fulfilled.

Question — Of course, we're all familiar with St. Paul's statement that "God is not mocked," and that whatsoever we sow we shall one day reap. But how can we possibly reconcile the terrible injustices in life with an all-loving God?

Comment — That's just the point. We can't reconcile them, if we limit the experience of the soul to one short span of seventy-odd years — for how could we then reap the effects of our sowing? No, the idea of rebirth is essentially one of hope, because it assures the inevitability of justice — in the course of time.

Question — I'd like to ask a question that has always troubled me. When we die, do we lose our personality? For example, will I recognize myself when I come back again?

Comment — You had no difficulty in recognizing your individuality this time, did you? No, you take yourself as you are, with all your strengths and all your weaknesses — they are as familiar to you as the very air you breathe, for the reason that you have grown through the ages with yourself. Still, the personality is not the real you, but only a mask you wear, and that mask has changed thousands and thousands of times as you have played your different roles in the long drama of experience. Thus when we die, we lose everything connected with the particular mask we have just worn; in other words, we lose our physical brain and body that we have used as Mary Brown or Joe Smith. However, the reincarnating element that uses Mary Brown or Joe Smith in any one lifetime will return again and again, each time taking on a new personality, a new brain and physical body, fresh and revitalized and exactly fitted by karma, through which to grow and learn the lessons of the new life. Why do you suppose it was said: "Ye are the temple of the living God" — a *living* God, working in and through our personalities?

Question — Just what is it that reincarnates then? Is it the divine spark or the living God?

Comment — The divine spark itself does not reincarnate, any more than the sun leaves its orbit of duty. Nevertheless, just as its warmth and light penetrate all layers of the atmospheres between the sun and the earth, so is it with man. The spark of godhood remains transcendent in its own divine orbit, yet its light or vital essence permeates our whole nature, focusing its force through the spiritual soul that it

41

may illumine the highest mental or truly human part, our higher self. It is that permanent, immortal element in us, therefore, which endures from life to life, reincarnating in a new personality with each birth on earth. But the divinity per se must have intermediaries or 'transformers' to step down its higher potency, and hence does not reincarnate directly. Still, the reincarnating element could no more exist or function apart from its divine parent than a sunbeam could exist or function apart from its solar parent, from which it streams to give life and substance, not alone to earth and all its creatures, but to the entire dominion of the solar system.

Question — For most of us the thought of developing a nearness to the Father within seems extremely remote. If we do reap what we sow, and I for one feel this to be true, then by inference we must have been reaping and sowing over a very long time. This in itself seems like a load that is almost too hard to bear — that for thousands of ages we have had to struggle on alone, making countless errors, sowing field upon field of "wild oats," without the strength and the knowledge to guide us.

Comment — But we haven't been alone, and we aren't alone now. When the divine spark within each one of us led us from the Garden of Eden, and said in essence: You have gone a long way up to this point, now you can earn the right to work out your destiny yourselves — that divinity did not leave us. It retired deep within our souls, and remains there today. Every day of our lives it is saying to us, if only we will listen: You are my prodigal son. Go your way, through what pain and suffering and joy you make for yourself. But remember from now on you must by your own free will travel the cycles of experience. Then when you win your way back to me, you will be strong and enriched — in fact, you will be a god like unto me.

That divine spark has never forsaken us, and never will; for its very nature is to radiate its influence until not only do we recognize its presence, but determine henceforth to work with and become like unto it.

No, we have never been alone, nor do we carry the whole load of past error in one lifetime; moreover, in our thousands of lifetimes, have we not also sown beautiful flowers and not merely tares in the garden of our soul? We need never feel that we cannot meet the pressures of ourselves: "God fits the burden to the shoulders"— which does not mean that the Divine Intelligence measures each one of us with a yardstick and gives us just so much and no more of a burden for today and tomorrow and the next day. It does not have to, because within each one of us is its individual representative, a spark of that all-encompassing Divinity which is our own immortal self, with whom ultimately we shall become fully acquainted. Thus it is in very truth our Father who acts as our protector, and allows us to handle only that portion of karma that we in our strength and immaturity are able to carry.

We can take courage in the knowledge that when our troubles seem more than we can bear, there is within us that guardianship that assures us the power and the wisdom to meet the challenge. The very fact that we are living today on earth is a proof, a magnificent proof, that we have not lost touch with our inner god — else we would not be here as learning, aspiring human souls.

43

Heredity and Environment

QUESTION — As I understand it, heredity and environment are the two principal factors involved in the theory of evolution. But then, if reincarnation is true, how does heredity fit in? We know that certain laws have been arrived at which prove physical heredity, and that environment also plays a major part in one's development. On the other hand, geniuses are sometimes born to illiterate families, so it seems that after you leave the physical plane the rules don't apply. When you delve into the matter of a man's soul, can you say he inherits from his parents his mental and emotional or spiritual characteristics?

Comment — Don't forget too the other factor in evolution that cannot be side-stepped: the matter of the fruitage of thoughts and acts that we have sown in previous lives. We come into life with a lot of unexpended karma which is bound to find an outlet some time, somewhere, on this earth — in an environment where those former seeds of character may find expression.

Question — It has been shown that the law of cause and effect governs physical heredity; for instance, if a black rabbit and a white rabbit are mated, the scientists can tell you exactly what the genes and chromosomes will do for the next ten generations. And now they are seeking to prove through the genes and the chromosomes that you also inherit from your parents your psychological and mental qualities; in fact, all the capabilities you possess. But surely this last point is open to serious question?

Comment — Nature usually follows one general rule: "As below, so above; as above, so below," as the Hermetic axiom puts it. Just because we don't know how the rules apply on the higher planes of our constitution doesn't necessarily mean that those rules change *in principle*. Their application on the physical plane may signify one thing, and on the mental another.

Now let us go back a little and look at heredity from the standpoint of more than one life. "A" is born to a certain couple. Physically, he will have certain characteristics that the father and mother have, or that are in the family stream. But why is "A" born to that family and to no other? Is it just by chance? No, "A" is born to that father and mother at that particular time and place, and under the specific circumstances that exist, which exactly fit the karma of the reincarnating element seeking birth. In my judgment, no child could possibly be born unless there was a strong magnetic pull or attraction — whether of love or hate — impelling that soul to come to its parents.

You could say then that "A" inherits from his own past the very qualities that his parents seem to provide through the medium of the physical elements, the genes and chromosomes, etc. But this doesn't tell you *why*, unless you recognize the part that the reincarnating element plays in coming into birth through the father and mother.

The rules do not change anywhere along the line, from the physical on up, or vice versa — they only seem to change because science can catalogue its observations on the material plane and work out certain deductions therefrom, but isn't able to catalogue the subtler aspects of the mind and soul.

Question — You mean, then, that although you pick out the father and mother who can give you what is similar to your own characteristics, you actually do inherit yourself?

Comment — Yes, that is exactly what I believe: each one inherits himself from his own past. Therefore, whether consciously or not, we 'select' our parents because of similarity of characteristics, or because they are diametrically opposite to what we are. Both love and hate are magnetic in their power to attract, and that is why sometimes children are born to parents where there is strong dislike or animosity between a child and one or both parents.

Question — As I understand it, our soul is what we have made of ourselves in the past?

47

Comment — A *portion* of what we have made of ourselves in the past.

Question — Yes. Then when we die, can we say that our soul goes into a kind of rest, withdraws into itself somewhat as a plant goes into a seed? I am trying to connect the soul or mental part of us with the physical body which starts out in life as a seed, and has its genes and chromosomes.

Comment — I see, and you have an excellent point there. It reminds me of the story from the *Upanishads*, where an old sage is telling his pupil about the indwelling spirit. He asks him to bring him a fruit from a large fig tree. "Break it open and tell me what you see." "Only these extremely fine seeds," replied the youth. "Now break open one of the seeds and tell me what you see." "Nothing at all," was the answer. The sage then pointed out that this "nothingness" is "the True, the Self," the imperceptible essence which causes the fruit or the tree and all manifested things to come into being; and that all else, the body of the fruit, the skin, pulp, etc., are merely the forms that the Self takes.

This, I believe, is the key to a fuller understanding of the mysterious and hidden support of the continuity of life. Each of us, like the fig tree, is the direct result of the activity of that indwelling spirit. Call it what you will — the Father within, the guardian angel, the monadic essence of being or that unknown something that gives pattern even to the DNA molecule — the fact remains that without this subtle core of ourselves we would be drifting without identification, without continuity, without life.

Question — Then would you say that the soul of the fig or of a man really goes into "nothingness" when it dies —

if we understand by "nothingness" a non-manifesting or sleeping stage? If the genes and chromosomes are the expression of the seed of the physical body, could there be a spiritual seed which is expressing itself as our personality or human ego? It seems to me it should be consistent right on through.

Comment — It is consistent in principle, though we cannot always see it working out. After you take away the pulp and the skin and even the kernel — what do you have? Nothing, nothingness. Yet we know that there is *something*, a "subtle essence," as the *Upanishad* calls it; there must be, or we wouldn't have the fruit, the tree, or the man. What is it? It is the consciousness, the seed-essence if you like. So when we die, you could say that the soul of a man becomes again a seed-consciousness. Certainly it is not of any material nature; you cannot associate physical matter with it at all.

Question — You say no "material nature" whatever. Do you mean that literally? I always thought that if you go far enough matter gets into spirit, and spirit into matter, or is it only a relative thing?

Comment — Speaking once again in principle, matter and spirit are one — two sides of a coin — because matter reduced to its elements is spirit, and spirit in manifestation is matter. But that does not mean that we should not differentiate between what is spiritual and what is material. To return to the seed-consciousness, whether of a plant or of a man: when that seed wants to manifest, it takes on materials of various levels or gradations so that it can express itself. But in its "nothingness" or in its seed-essence it is consciousness, spirit, in various degrees of tenuousness. Of course, you can-

49

not say that consciousness is nothingness — for consciousness is the most vitally alive part, actually the seed-essence
of divinity which is only a seeming nothingness judged from
the material point of view. But let's not get too far afield.

Question — Where does parental heredity begin, and
where does it leave off and other factors enter in?

Question — Could we link this up with the mental and
emotional aspects? It was stated a while ago that the mother
and father provide the physical vehicle. Well, let us suppose
the mother and father also have emotional or mental characteristics that would tend to bring about a certain type of
result, say either a genius or an idiot, or a stable or unstable
character. Could we say that the incoming child chooses
his parents not only for a physical body, but also for the
emotional and mental and psychological capacities that fit
in with his karma?

Comment — Generally speaking, you are right, but we
must always take into consideration that in the human kingdom the factors of free will and the higher level of consciousness operate over and above the physical transmission
of genes and chromosomes. Nor should we lose sight of the
fact that in any one lifetime we could not possibly meet the
whole of our karmic responsibilities. We can handle only a
small share of them in the normal span of life.

It matters little into what race or family or nation a child
may be born. When the thirst for life begins in the consciousness of the child-to-be, then the inner impulses begin
to stir, to awaken from their resting-place, and push the soul
out of its heaven-world into another experience on earth.
The seed-essence, the spiritual and the higher mental con-

sciousness, attract by karma the psychological and physical elements that are needed to fulfill the specific type of responsibility for the new life.

Question — In other words, the soul is attracted to those parents from whom it can inherit the necessary physical and emotional and mental traits?

Comment — I don't like to use the word inherit as it is at present scientifically used. It is too limiting. Rather let us say that the soul is attracted to those parents who can or will act as the medium for providing the vehicle and environment. They do not *provide* the vehicle, but they are definitely the means whereby the physical right on up to the higher mental and spiritual aspects can manifest. But *you 'inherit' yourself*, because you are yourself from out of the long past ages of experience.

Let us take the mystery of the union of the two infinitesimal cells at conception. Thousands of cells are thrown off from the father, but one, just one out of countless others, unites with a cell from the mother, and that marvelous process of embryonic growth starts. The parents don't form the embryo; nor do they make it grow. The mystery of growth takes place because the soul-essence of the child-to-be — the "nothingness" which made the fig become a fig — guides the growth of the foetus from conception on until sufficient of the life-atoms that formerly were his from past ages have been attracted to it. Now those life-atoms are his; the parents are not providing them. They are only being the medium through which those life-atoms are attracted to that combination of elements that is going to manifest as a human being when born on this earth.

Question — What do you mean by life-atoms?

Comment — Exactly what the term implies — the *life*-principle or vitalizing essence within the atomic particles that exist on every plane.

Question — What about the transmission of characteristics that obviously are passed on from generation to generation?

Comment — All that we observe as heredity is nothing more nor less than the process of a reimbodying human ego bringing itself into being in any lifetime through the channel of parents sympathetic to itself in certain of its characteristics. The several children in a large family, for instance, are each different and yet all show qualities common to the family stream. In other words, the incoming soul utilizes the family karma for its means of expression; but the parents don't create that child, physically, mentally or spiritually. What they provide is the environmental stage-setting. Each one of us has a large reserve of karmic energy which in one life will take this avenue, and in another that. It may be that you or I will need something completely different in experience next life from what we are meeting now, in order to balance the pattern of growth that we require to bring us nearer the goal — the goal for all of us being conscious co-operation with our higher selves.

We could summarize and say that heredity as propounded is nothing more than observations of a portion of life's greater pattern which, when classified by science, appear to be laws in themselves but actually, when viewed from the standpoint of the individual, are but one small part of the whole.

To talk about heredity as though it were the complete picture is like looking at a gorgeous landscape through a tiny slit. While the divine facet of our nature takes very little noticeable part, nevertheless it is the originating cause; the human ego being the responsible agent in our present stage of growth. Naturally scientists concentrate on the physical characteristics which they have catalogued to a nicety; but they forget that those physical and even mental and emotional characteristics would have no existence were it not for the indwelling spirit. It is that, the seed-essence, which is responsible for starting the whole chain of action which brings a soul into earth life.

Life does not continue to exist upon nothing. It exists upon itself, just as the fig tree exists upon the unseen essence within its seed. And who can say that we humans do not follow a similar sequence: birth of the soul, growth to maturity, death, assimilation of our experiences, rest and rejuvenation, a renewed thirst for life and, in due course, gestation and rebirth — to pick up again the task of continuity in which all of nature participates.

Bridge of Understanding

IN THE PRESENTATION of the age-old doctrines of cosmology and the laws of man, we should remember that none of the world teachers had in mind the founding of a great and powerful organization. The teachings they gave were fresh from the source, and everything that springs from this source encourages unselfish development. They did not offer a prescribed set of dogmas, but a living philosophy for the simple man, workable in the daily affairs of the round of life. It was only in the course of hundreds of years that many of the fundamental keys were hidden, if not lost. In spite of this, we can recognize if we are unbiased that the

55

keys to these universal doctrines are there — in the Christian Scriptures as well as in all sacred writings. Whereas most of the dogmas taught in the temples and churches are accepted literally by their devotees, we find many individuals seeking beneath the outer forms, seeking for the *kernel* of the original truth.

That is why it is important to pursue an intelligent study of comparative religions — not simply as an intellectual activity, but primarily to form a bridge of understanding between the peoples of all faiths. Much effort is being expended today in various countries toward economic and political cooperation, and a certain amount toward a recognition of spiritual foundations. But we will never bridge the gap unless we recognize that our brother, regardless of the color of his skin or the nation or continent in which he found birth, has as much right to truth as we, and that his religion at heart may be just as broad and as universal as our own.

Our interest must start with the individual: to try to help him to help himself. We all need to develop discrimination in recognizing the qualities that are being expressed through the consciousness of another. If we understand the basis of his belief, we can talk to him in his own language. That in itself immediately makes a bridge of understanding between his heart and ours. With understanding comes confidence, and once mutual confidence is established, there will be born a trust. And when trust comes, the solution of our most difficult problems is made easy.

This will not happen overnight. One person may receive genuine inspiration from church services, another may not. But whether we go to church or not, whether we are Christian, Buddhist or Moslem, or whether we have developed our own philosophy of life, the fact remains that truth is to be had. The more we can study the ancient religions and think about them, the more we will expand our consciousness and find the same underlying truths because, as said, all of them came from the one Source, and each has its esoteric as well as its exoteric background.

When we speak of the church, or any other organized spiritual effort, we must be careful to distinguish between the institution and its members. Whatever their belief, most individuals are sincere and honest, but sincerity and honesty alone do not make a thing spiritual. One can be a hundred percent devoted and true in his heart, but still not be on the right track. The Inquisition of European history is witness to devotion and honesty prostituted to fanaticism and intrigue.

What then is the common denominator in spiritual issues? Certainly not the outer forms, the creeds or dogmas that have been grafted like barnacles onto world thought. Is it not a belief in some form of God, or Divine Power, that is the mainspring of our universe, and all that in it lives? Whether we worship Christ, Buddha or Allah, Brahmā, Vishnu or Śiva, Tao, Elohim or Jehovah, we instinctively recognize Deity as our fount and origin, and hopefully as our ultimate goal.

Now, if we can conceive of the essence of Deity, of the tremendous Divinity that pervades not only this solar system, but all the other solar universes that the astronomers tell us are within our own Milky Way, and within all the millions of Milky Ways, we will begin to see what this concept of God is, how undefinable, how illimitable.

Most certainly God resides within the heart of each one.

57

Not that we are God, but within the very deepest parts of the human soul, which goes far beyond the physical body, there is what may be called a god-spark, a spark of that Divinity which governs the cosmos. The entire purpose of evolution is to unfold that god-spark so that in the natural process of time and experience it will affect and transmute our whole constitution. "He who seeks shall find. Knock and it shall be opened unto you." There is not an individual on the face of the earth who will not find the answer to life's riddle if he honestly wants to. No one can do it for another. Every real step of progress for the race must begin with each one of us, from the point where we stand. We don't have to wait until we have become perfect; because it is never difficult to see where we need to work on ourselves, and where we have a natural opportunity to help others. For when a person turns inward for strength and guidance, the results that follow will be truly beneficial.

Once we recognize that each man's concept of God is different, but that the quality of Deity is the same and that the Divine essence resides in the core of all that lives, then we have laid the foundation upon which to build a bridge of brotherhood over which man can travel from the darkness of past ages to the light of the future.

The great religions all teach the priority of
spiritual over material riches. They
all teach the worth of the individual and
his capacity to grow nearer to God. And they
all agree on the principle of unity, the
unity of the universe, the unity of the human
family. To this unity all men are taught
that they belong. To help make progress
toward it is a personal contribution
that must come from each of us.

— EDWARD R. MURROW

The Golden Rule

THE STRONG souls coming to birth these days are storming
the barriers of doctrinal theology. Many of them will join
the great number of the "unchurched" who, while not adhering to any denominational regimen, are yet not to be
classed as "atheists," but rather as those who prefer to find
their God in the quiet of their own souls. For out of the
heart come the issues of life, and when men and women

everywhere seriously try to penetrate to the roots of spiritual issues, the quality of their faith will outdistance the patterned 'faith' of creeds. Despite diversities, we all share a common heritage, as instanced in the universal expression of the Golden Rule — a spiritual courtesy whose guidance could greatly diminish the ills of our civilization:

American Indian:

Great Spirit, grant that I may not criticize my neighbor until I have walked a mile in his moccasins.

Buddhism:

In five ways should a clansman minister to his friends and familiars — by generosity, courtesy, benevolence, by treating them as he treats himself, and by being as good as his word.

Christianity:

All things whatsoever ye would that men should do to you, do ye even so to them: for this is the law and the prophets.

Confucianism:

"Is there any one word," asked Tzŭ Kung, "which could be adopted as a lifelong rule of conduct?" The Master replied: "Is not Sympathy the word? Do not do to others what you would not like yourself."

Greek Philosophy:

Do not do to others what you would not wish to suffer yourself. — ISOCRATES

Treat your friends as you would want them to treat you. — ARISTOTLE

Hinduism:

One should not behave towards others in a way which is disagreeable to oneself. This is the essence of duty (dharma). All else results from selfish desire.

Islam:

No one of you is a believer until he loves for his brother what he loves for himself.

Judaism:

Thou shalt not hate thy brother in thine heart: ... but thou shalt love thy neighbor as thyself.

Zoroastrianism:

That nature only is good when it shall not do unto another whatever is not good for its own self.

When a sufficient number of liberated thinkers give open expression to their innermost beliefs, we shall find that the brotherhood of thought now in process will provide such a bulwark of spiritual strength that no storms of national differences will prevail, and emancipation from separatism will be assured.

Three Pillars of Ancient Tradition

QUESTION — For some years now the various world religions have been receiving increasing attention in popular books and magazines, and the basic tenets are often outlined in comparison with our Christian Scriptures. However, I find it somewhat confusing. It is simple enough to see the similarity in the ethics of the different faiths, the Golden Rule, the fatherhood of God, and so forth; but in all this welter of beliefs, rituals and legends I hardly know what I believe now.

Comment — Does your thought come down to this: is there any touchstone by which we can test the validity of any belief, whatever its source?

Question — Yes. How can we judge what is true, and what isn't?

Comment — This desire to understand the religious roots of others is one of the most encouraging signposts of the century, yet our very eagerness to reach out and embrace every concept and ideology, just because it is different from our own, poses a real danger. In fact, you have put your finger on both the strength and the weakness of the present awakening interest in the beliefs of others, for one of the greatest obstacles to solid growth is the tendency to accept this or that person, or this or that presentation, as authoritative. The last word has not been said, either in philosophy or religion, and certainly not in science. Nor could it be said, else there would be no chance for individual progress. There is no definitive statement on truth. But that does not mean that truth does not exist, nor that we human beings are unable to discover it.

What is truth? It is like the horizon that ever eludes us but is always before us. When we want to know what is beyond the horizon, we travel the road that leads toward it. But when we arrive, the horizon has moved on; and it will always move on. Just so with truth: we shall never reach the "last horizon," because there will always be another and another.

Ever since man became self-conscious, he has been searching for that Something that would yield him a clearer glimpse of reality. Call it the Holy Grail, the Philosopher's Stone or the Golden Fleece — always this hunger has kept alive his will to search. That is why the great religions have persisted, some of them for thousands of years, because no matter what form they have taken, underlying nearly every dogma and ritual is a vein of truth. The deeper we go into the roots of the different faiths, the more surely do we recognize their common ground.

Why would that be? The closer we penetrate to their origins the simpler and purer the teachings, and the more similar they are to each other. The farther back we delve into pre-history, the nearer we approach certain spiritual principles which have been handed down through the ages as a sacred tradition. There is good reason to believe, therefore, that at a very early period great Ideas were implanted in the consciousness of infant humanity, which later were universally broadcast among all peoples of the earth. But so heavy have been the credal trappings that it is difficult to uncover the original ancient tradition. Nevertheless, every great religion has drawn from it both for content and inspiration. It was the foundation too of the instruction and training of the old Mystery-schools of Greece and Asia Minor, Egypt and of India. It has likewise been called the wisdom-religion of antiquity.

Question — In order to find the oneness of all these faiths, wouldn't we have to do a tremendous amount of study and research?

Comment — Not necessarily. While the principles of this tradition may seem rather abstruse and verging on high philosophy, yet when analyzed we discover they are very near to our own daily experience, and thus quite understandable.

Who of us, for example, has not pondered on the mystery of God, and how his influence can penetrate everywhere at one and the same time? When we look up into the stars and see the Milky Way with its dark patches and its brilliant clusters, is it not the greatest of mysteries? Our scientists are pushing space farther and farther into infinity, as they discover more and more universes similar to our own. The inevitable question comes: what is Space? And the answer: it is endless, and it is beginningless. Then when we consider what the scientists call novae as well as proto-stars, by which they describe stars which apparently are disappearing and the new stellar matter which is becoming stars, we cannot help but realize that everywhere there is an eternal rhythm and movement.

Let me try now to give in simple outline the three fundamental postulates as presented by H. P. Blavatsky in *The Secret Doctrine*, and upon which this ancient theosophia or wisdom-religion rests. We can discuss them afterwards. The first is:

That behind everything in the universe there is the Unknowable, the vast abyss of Space, Reality. Impossible to describe, we call it simply Infinity, without beginning, without end, because it is without attributes or finite qualities. Many names have been given in an attempt to describe the Boundless, but man cannot define the Indefinable. The Old Testament writers spoke of it as "without form and void," and as the "Darkness upon the face of the deep." The Buddhists also called it the Void or Emptiness, because nothing as yet had taken form. In the Icelandic *Eddas*, the old Norse bards named it the "Yawning Gap"; while in the *Zohar* the Kabbalists used the term *Ein Soph*, meaning "without limits" or the "boundless."

From this seeming No-thing-ness — which was not nothingness at all, but a condition of latency vibrant with expectant life, the seed-essences of divinity — the second basic concept follows:

That motion, rhythm, or the periodic appearance of a Universe from the Darkness of the Boundless into the Light, is the action of Deity as it bursts through into manifestation — a word which implies a period of activity as contrasted with the condition of quiescence in which it had been during its period of rest. As an ancient stanza has it: like the ebb and flux of the tides, numberless universes called "sparks of Eternity" come and go, appear and disappear, with all that is contained therein. We are familiar with this law of periodicity, for the rhythm of nature's cycles is seen in the alternation of day and night, birth and death, waking and sleeping, the waxing and waning of the moon, and the cycle of the four seasons.

Question — Are we, as human beings, then bound by this law of ebb and flux? Where does our free will come in? It looks as though we have to come out of Darkness into active life when a universe does; and if so, how does our own individual evolution fit into the greater picture?

Comment — We are all bound by the laws of nature, fortunately, insofar as our general growth and progress are concerned. As a part of the Whole, naturally we must follow the over-all pattern of that Whole; though how we weave our individual pattern within the greater is our responsibility. But before we go further, let me outline briefly the third principle because it touches on the very points you bring up.

Following upon the first and second principles — that of Darkness upon the face of the deep, and the bursting forth into Light of universes-to-be — the third asserts: "the fundamental identity of all souls with the Universal Over-soul," to use Emerson's term. This simply means that every aspect of a universe, from galaxies to man and on down through the lower kingdoms, is identic *in essence* with God or the Universal Divine Intelligence.

Question — You mean we are identic because we all partake of God?

Comment — Identic in essence, yes; but not in expression, because we are all individual god-sparks of the One Intelligence. But there is more to this third principle:

When the universe is breathed forth out of its latent condition, out of Darkness, it and all the potential seeds of life within it feel the impelling force to start another cycle of active growth. Therefore each entity, by the very force of the evolutionary urge, has to pass through every phase of experience, including mineral, plant and animal forms, until the human kingdom is reached. From then on, these god-sparks must by their own efforts unfold their essential divinity, so that in time they will have earned the right to become truly self-conscious gods.

It is a long pilgrimage, sometimes called the "Cycle of Necessity" because it suggests that the entire process of evolution takes in the necessity to grow, to evolve, to benefit by all that nature throughout her kingdoms has to offer. As "sparks of Eternity" we have had to enrich our store of experience by *using* mineral, plant and animal bodies — but only as temporary media of expression. God does not *become*

68

the stone or the vegetable, but an aspect of the Divine *is* the focal center of every stone or plant or animal. Just as we cannot say that our inner god *is* a human being, but only uses our human vehicle as its present means of self-expression, so we cannot say that we as *human beings* were ever minerals, plants or animals. This is a most important distinction to make.

Question — I was able to follow you for the most part, but it would be helpful if you could give a brief summary.

Comment — This whole picture is so vast and, while the principles are simple in their essentials, their ramifications can become exceedingly complex. Let me try again.

First, there is the great Void, Darkness upon the deep, before the "creation" of Heaven and earth — only Infinity, boundless, frontierless, Space, the Unknowable, without attributes or qualities. Then, like the surging of a Great Breath, Divinity stirs, the "spirit of God" moves on the face of the waters, and a universe comes into being. Third, all the gradations of living entities within the encompassing field of a universe, from the farthest star to the lowliest atom, are individual expressions of Deity; and thus every facet of that universe, bearing the stamp of godhood, now has not only the opportunity but the duty to become in time self-consciously godlike. And so every god-spark enters upon its long evolutionary journey through all of nature's kingdoms, and finally, as a fully developed god it, with the universe, ends its period of activity and is indrawn into a period of rest.

Question — That is wonderful. But where does God fit into this scheme?

Comment — It depends on your concept of God. I don't suppose any two of us think of God in quite the same way.

Question — I don't believe in God as a Person with supreme totalitarian power, able to grant every wish. I really don't know what I do think about God. It is so difficult to express these things, because we have been taught consistently since childhood to conceive of God as a kind of Being, and no matter how enlarged our concept He still is more or less a Person. I like the idea of everything being an aspect of God, but could you place God in relation to all that you have been saying?

Comment — We shouldn't try too hard to get all these ideas systematically arranged in our minds, with God here, Space over there, and matter somewhere else. This question of God varies so greatly in the different faiths and philosophies that it is sometimes difficult to make a relation between one concept of God and another.

Everything is in God, and God is in everything, yet it is not any thing. Nowhere in the Christian Scriptures, properly interpreted, do we find God mentioned in a limiting personal sense. The Scriptures speak of Gods, Elohim, but not of God. At no time did the Old Testament writers name Deity; they mention some seventy-seven different names of God, which they frankly recognize as seventy-seven different attributes, but they never define what God is. They go all around the subject to draw out the spiritual force of what they felt God was, but they never name him. The truth of the matter is that they did not want to, because they knew they could never confine the spirit of the Illimitable within the boundary of a name.

Other peoples following other lines of spiritual development have used different terminology. Sir James Jeans in one of his most popular books, *The Mysterious Universe*, conceived of God as a great mathematician, suggesting that all manifestation was an expression of a great thought.

One of our difficulties stems from the misapplication of our birthright: although *Genesis* specifically says that the Lord God made man in his image, we have reversed the procedure and given God human qualities, only trying to make them God-size!

Let us get away from all such limiting concepts, and consider God as the Divine Intelligence which is the root and origin of all that lives and moves. At the heart of a tree is God, but God is not the tree; at the core of every tiniest atom throughout the fields of space God is, but God is not the atom. So with man. God is not a human being, but a human being could not exist were he not rooted in God. So you and I, as "aspects of God," portions of this Divine Intelligence, are truly parts of God, and one day will realize this in fullness.

Question — What, then, is the relation between God and the Unknowable, or this first principle that you also called the Boundless?

Comment — When we speak of the Unknowable, we have to try to reach out with our imagination to Infinity — an impossibility of course, nevertheless only by so doing will we even come close to an understanding of just what the Unknowable is. It is the Void, but it is also, as the ancient Greeks called it, the Pleroma, the "Fullness" — and literally that, because it is pregnant with the seeds of universes-to-be.

Question — Earlier you used the phrase, "vibrant with expectant life." Is that what you mean here?

Comment — Exactly. What is the relation then between God and the Unknowable? We might say that the Boundless, the Unknowable, is God quiescent (at least from *our* viewpoint), while the moment activity is conceived and manifestation begins, the once sleeping god-sparks stir into life. Thus as soon as the first quiver of vitality is felt, trillions of these god-sparks, like a great outrushing of the Breath of Divinity, burst through from latency into activity, from Darkness into Light. Thereafter, all the various types of these god-sparks begin their evolutionary trek, impelled by necessity or karma as they pass through nature's kingdoms. Once the human kingdom is reached, and self-consciousness is acquired, then slowly these god-sparks must work their way through the university of life and graduate as gods.

Question — It looks as though we have an awfully long pull ahead of us before we come anywhere near to becoming godlike! How much free will do we have, or are we compelled to follow this "Cycle of Necessity"?

Comment — Of course we have the power of choice and freedom of will, within the broad limits of universal law. While it is true that during the period when the god-sparks were using mineral bodies, and later plant and animal forms, they gained their experience more or less automatically, because carried along by the great impulsion of the forward moving stream of life; still, once they manifested in human bodies, another factor entered the picture — the lighting of the fires of Mind in infant humanity. This is one of the most beautiful episodes in the spiritual history of man. Whatever name we care to give those "Light-bringers," every world scripture has preserved knowledge of their sacred function, though this has through centuries of limited and personalized interpretation taken on an entirely false significance. Far from being a serpent of evil, the Fallen Angel or Lucifer was truly a "Light-bringer" — a Prometheus whose daring brought the flaming ember from the gods in order that self-conscious contact with our sleeping god-spark might bring to man awareness of his innate godhood. This is the real meaning of the story of *Genesis*. It is all there.

If we remember nothing else, let us keep in mind this one grand idea: that even the most minute element is an expression of the Divine Intelligence, a differentiation of the essence of the Unknowable, and that through the long cycles of experience the opportunity will be given for each god-essence to return again unto its Father, enriched by its sojourn through all the kingdoms of nature, both below the human and above. In a very real sense, this is the parable of the Prodigal Son, who after manifold experiences in the spheres of matter finally yearns for the things of his Father. Returning then to his Home, great is the rejoicing, for one more god-spark has overcome the pull of matter and earned conscious reunion with his abiding Divinity.

It is a wondrous picture, and once we grasp these three principles or fundamentals of the wisdom-religion, we realize that they do indeed form a touchstone upon which we can test the many conflicting concepts of the peoples of every faith.

73

God, God's Will and Predestination

$\bigcirc$ UESTION — There are so many questions we'd like to discuss with you — about God, and free will, and Adam's Fall, that we don't know where to start. Of course we can say everything is "the will of God," and for some in our group that is enough, perhaps because they have more trust than I. But I would like to ask, what is your creed or formula of belief?

Comment — Before I say anything else, let me make one thing clear: as far as I am concerned, you and I, and every-

75

one, are all searchers for truth. It matters little whether a person is twenty, fifty or eighty years of age — we all seek knowledge and understanding in our own individual way. Therefore no one has the right to speak with 'final authority' on truth, or to attempt to give the last word on the laws of nature.

You ask, what is my creed or formula of belief? I have no creed, no organized formula of faith, no dogma of belief. Just as every blade of grass is different, so every human being is different. While the principles of truth are unchanging, the manner in which those principles have found expression has varied considerably with every world teacher. This is not only natural; it is essential to growth, for one of the most prevalent tendencies in human nature is the inclination to crystallize, to settle down comfortably with a tidy set of beliefs, and think: "Now, at last, I have the truth. There is no need to worry any longer about seeking it." That attitude is to me one of the greatest stumbling blocks to the spiritual progress of anyone sincerely seeking to expand his understanding of life.

I don't like the word creed one bit, for the reason that it usually connotes an authoritative summary of religious doctrine, or some formal statement of faith. That is precisely what I object to — regardless of how lofty or true such may be. The most important thing in my opinion is not the attainment of truth (or of any aspect of it, since we never could arrive at truth per se), but the searching after and the reaching toward a greater and greater understanding of it. If I had to have a creed, that would be it: the absolute conviction of the soul's need for a *free* avenue of research within its own range of consciousness.

76

Question — But you must believe in something. For example, do you believe in Jesus?

Comment — Certainly I believe in Jesus — though not necessarily as you do. I believe that Jesus was an incarnation of a Divine force, God if you prefer. But I also believe that Jesus was not unique in this, because every man potentially is a "son of God," an incarnation of his own inner divinity. Did not Jesus say to us that what he did we could do also, and even greater things? What did he mean by this except to remind us that we too are "temples of the Most High"? Those were not mere words of comfort; in them he left a message of immense hope and confidence in the spiritual destiny of man.

Question — You seem to believe in God, but would you tell us exactly how you feel about Him?

Comment — Do I believe in God? That all depends upon what you mean by God. If you mean, do I believe in a Personal God, a Deity outside of man, then I would have to say that my belief in God extends far beyond the usual orthodox view. God has become for me that Divine Intelligence which is the background and foreground of all creation. In other words, to my mind nothing could exist except it were a part of God, an expression of that divine force. Using our Christian terminology, this is what seems true to me:

First, that the Waters of Space of *Genesis* not only are boundless and infinite, but are the divine Source of all manifested creatures; second, that when God or the Elohim breathed on the Waters of Space the Void became a Fullness, and God burst forth from the Darkness on the face of

77

the deep into Light — and a universe with its hosts of life forms came into being. And third, that because the Elohim (to use again the Hebrew term for Gods plural, not God singular) impregnated every atom of Space with the divine essence, every facet of the universe must be an expression, however infinitesimal, of God — which means, further, that every creature in the heavens and the earth has the opportunity to become self-consciously godlike. Obviously such self-conscious at-one-ment with God isn't accomplished in a day, but must take long ages through time and space until every aspect of God has had the chance to find expression in all the kingdoms. Then when the Great Day comes, all that was emanated from the Darkness of the Void will once again be indrawn into the bosom of God for its period of rest.

Question — When you say it like that, it makes everything so big, so awesome. It almost scares me, though, because it's hard to get back into the orthodox view if you really let yourself go along those lines. You've made it pretty clear, however, that your school of thought isn't trying to replace anything that we've been taught.

Comment — I am glad you expressed yourself just as you did, because the intent is not to replace anyone's beliefs, but rather to try to help an individual interpret his own faith in a fuller and richer way. The only 'dogma' that I adhere to is that there should be no dogmatization of thought. Truth is open to all, but the way thereto is a strictly individual affair. We shouldn't take anything as true unless it feels right deep down inside. Tomorrow any one of us may see things quite differently, have a greater understanding than we have today. Then today's belief will seem limited. So it is with growth on every plane of experience.

Question — I like that, because the one thing I can't abide is to have somebody say: "Now this is the way things are, and that is all there is to it." I don't think anybody has the right to say that. So I have just been plodding along, trying to pick up what I could, a little here and a little there. I suppose everyone can have his own brand of truth. Is it possible that certain ideas in our Christian belief are somewhat similar to other beliefs?

Comment — Not only is it possible, but you are absolutely right; and as you study the world's great religions and philosophies, both of the Occident and the Orient, you will find that all of them spring from a common source. The Christian Scriptures contain many of the same doctrines that Buddhism and Hinduism teach, though differently expressed; so too can you trace in the Gospels Hebrew and Greek influences. All postulate a divine source, whether called Jehovah, Brahmā or Allah; the special Incarnation of God or Deity through Christ is directly parallel to the Hindu Avatāras; and, as we know, the Golden Rule of moral and spiritual behavior is universally found. But just as with our Christian faith much dogmatism has entered in, so is this the case with the Eastern beliefs, and it is not always easy to see through these distortions.

Through comparison of the literatures, myths and traditions of other lands, we discover that the Creation story of *Genesis*, for example, is but one aspect of a universal tale, sacredly preserved in one form or another by every people the world over, whether civilized or primitive. Even though

79

scientific and archaeological discovery has proved beyond the shadow of a doubt that our earth is millions of years old instead of a mere 6,000 years, these Creation stories are not mere fantasy or childish imaginings. But how explain the creation of the heaven and the earth in six days, with God resting on the seventh! Taken literally, it is absurd; but it was never so intended. The Days of Creation, whether of the Christian Bible or of the Hindu Purānas, the American Indian legends or the Persian, are meant to symbolize Days of manifestation or activity, followed by Nights of withdrawal or rest — each of these Days being a life-cycle of terrestrial experience, ranging from a few thousand to perhaps hundreds of thousands of years.

All of which leads us to the conclusion that man too must be very, very old. In fact, some scriptures assert that at least eighteen million years have elapsed since he became a self-conscious unit! Whatever his age, whether millions of years or only a few thousands, the fact remains that it has been the untiring effort of all the great spiritual reformers of the ages to help us grasp the larger picture of man's divine potential.

Question — If every one of us, as you said, is an "incarnation of God," at least in degree; and if when God breathed on the Waters we all came into being, don't we have to go through all sorts of experience before we can join God again? But what happens between the first and the last step? How does it work out from the beginning until the end?

Comment — As far as I know, there is only one process, one *modus operandi* of becoming like unto the god within, and that is through repetitive experiences until we learn completely the lessons that our earth has for us.

Question — Are you referring to reincarnation? I was reared in a very orthodox family, and it's difficult for me to accept the idea. Still I can't quite throw it out, so I wish you'd say more about it.

Comment — There is no need for anyone to believe in reincarnation. On the other hand, there is no need to be afraid of a new idea. But I will say this: the concept of re-birth is a very ancient one and can be recognized in every religion, even the Christian, despite the fact that great pains were taken in the early centuries to remove it as one of the cardinal doctrines of the Church.

For purposes of discussion, let us assume that the soul might need more time than just the seventy-odd years usually allotted to it. How would it manage this, if death ends all? I believe we will readily admit that we cannot fulfill one tenth of our deepest hopes in so short a period. Now let us assume further that in his divine wisdom God allows us another chance, another opportunity for develop-ment. Would it be sensible to go anywhere else but here on earth where we had already become somewhat familiar with this planet and its laws? There is another point equally important: haven't we set a number of causes in motion already and, if so, do we really believe we can reap the consequences of all our thoughts and acts before we die?

Question — I have always thought that things are sup-posed to be a certain way, that nothing happens by chance. Yet I have also felt that man has a free will. I guess after all

I am a fatalist, and yet I like to think we have some freedom of choice too.

Comment — I don't think you are really a fatalist, but let me try to re-express the picture as I see it, without getting too far afield. If we believe that the law of cause and effect works not only physically but in our moral and spiritual relations as well, and that what we sow in the field of our soul we will have to reap somewhere at some time, then we see that nothing could "just happen" by chance, or contrary to the laws of nature. Yet this law of harmony is so delicately balanced that each individual finds it manifesting in a different manner, precisely according to his own soul-background.

Question — What do you mean by "soul-background"? Is the soul the same as the spirit?

Comment — Perhaps before I go further I had better briefly comment on this point concerning the soul. You are all familiar with St. Paul's division of man into three: body, soul and spirit. Now it is difficult for many people to understand that the soul and the spirit are not the same; but they are not. You and I are human souls, gaining experience here in a physical body, but we are directed or urged into this experience by the spirit that resides within us. I am sure none of you believes that your body is you; or that even your emotions and brain or soul are all there is to you. What motivates your aspirations, your deepest feelings, unless it is your divine spark, that essence of God which is at the root of every living organism? So, let us think then of the permanent part of us as the spirit, stirring into action the human soul, which again uses a physical body as its temple here on earth.

Now that permanent element in us has managed to guide us into the positions in life from which we may learn the most. Yet as each of us is a facet of the Divine Intelligence, with our own portion of free will, it is up to us to exercise the right of choice, to choose which path to take, what thoughts to entertain, what actions to perform. You can see therefore that the soul stands on a battleground between spirit and body, between aspiration toward God on the one hand, and material desire on the other. Ours is an animal body, a highly developed one, but still it comes from the matter side of nature. Our soul partakes of strength from above, the god in man, but it also is sensitive to the pull of our physical nature. Here is where we have freedom of choice and also where we learn.

Question — I don't see how we can get around the idea of fatalism or predestination. Doesn't God have a will for our lives? And when we don't follow it, then we aren't in His will and have to search it out, don't we?

Comment — In one sense, and a very true one, we are all bound by God's will, provided we think of God as that portion of Deity which is at the heart of each one of us. That means that within us is the strength and potency of God's will which can in time be made manifest. But, and this is the important point, it will manifest differently for each individual, because it is the will of our *own* inner god whose divine force is impinging upon our soul. In that sense you could rightly say that man is "predestined" by his own inner god: to come into life and to experience the pain and pleasure of earthly existence.

But let us not confuse this with the old dogma that

83

asserted that man is preordained before birth to suffer punishment or reward, according to the whim or caprice of an extracosmic Deity. No man is predestined or preordained by any God outside of himself. Nor could he be predestined by anything other than the force of his own past experiences, the energies stored up by himself in the permanent portion of his being. In other words, man comes into life "preordained" by himself, and himself alone, to unfold and develop that which he has accumulated in his own soul-life; also stored there is his own individual quality of free will which he can utilize to make of himself whatever he chooses. We are prone to become fatalists because for centuries we have tended to view life and the circumstances around us through the narrow perspective of one lifetime. But once man awakens to a self-conscious knowledge of his full humanhood and responsibility, then fatalism is out of the picture.

Can any one of you possibly believe that you were "born in sin" literally, and that you are preordained to error unless God so wills it that you shall follow goodness? If we approach the question solely from the standpoint of the body, we could say that man is "born in sin" — if we mean by this born into matter, into a material animal body. But man is not his body. The soul is free, as near to freedom as it is near to its own innate godhood. That is the great challenge: man has within him the power through his portion of free will to become the willing helper of his own inner god.

Good and Evil

Q<small>UESTION</small> – I'm still unsatisfied about the matter of God's will and predetermination. How much leeway am I allowed, or am I absolutely bound by the will of God?

Comment – In the ultimate sense, every entity in space is within the realm of the divine will, under the impulsion of the divine energies that flow through and permeate the universe. We are not the marionettes of some all-powerful personal God, but free-willing agents, however unconscious we still are of our innate potential. Yet while each has a unique destiny, no man is an island apart and distinct from every other, but part of a great continent of experience and growth that encompasses the whole of humanity.

But how far you will be allowed to go off course, just how wide is your stretch of deviation — that I cannot answer for you. No one could. The only one who can answer that is yourself. We all make mistakes again and again, but that is not the deciding factor. What counts is the motive of our lives — the quality of aspiration that governs the whole of our thoughts and acts. However, we play with fire the moment we try to figure out just how far we can go wrong and "still get away with it."

Question — I didn't mean it that way. This is what I had in mind. Yesterday several of us were in Los Angeles for the ball game, and we had to wait quite a while before catching our bus home. Skid Row, as you know, is not far from the bus terminal; you see all sorts of people there, and you can't help wondering how they ever got so low down. Then you think to yourself, "But for the grace of God, there go I." I had always felt that no one would be permitted to get so far out of line, even with our free will, because I figured there would be something that would predetermine our going just so far and no farther. But there apparently wasn't anything to stop *those* people. That is where it is difficult to discern the line of cleavage between fatalism and free will. So my question is: how far can one go without having some kind of brakes take hold?

Comment — Anyone can go completely off course, if that is what he wants to do more than anything else. Fortunately, there is generally plenty of interference somewhere along the line, usually from within. Not only do we have our conscience, and a lively one once we start to heed it, but we likewise have the continuous presence of our guardian angel, which protects us more often than we know. How far can we go without having the brakes take hold? Just as far as our conscience will allow. We are perfectly aware when we go against that warning voice, which will never tell us what to do but will always stand ready to give us a "prick" when we even so much as think about doing something that for us, individually, would be a deviation from our true course.

Question — Would you call conscience then an instrumentality of God's will?

Comment — You could say that conscience is an instrumentality or working tool of the god within, for if the voice of conscience is born of long ages of trial and error, it must be closely linked with the tireless effort of the god part of ourselves to bring us into line with its divine will. Moreover, we are as near to our guardian angel as we are near to our own skin; but this relationship is two-way. Unless we earn that protection, we shall not receive it. "God is not mocked: for whatsoever a man soweth, that shall he also reap." It is the very reaping of sorrow and pain, of frustration and loneliness, that is the surest brake against our going too far downhill. But when a person deliberately chooses to stifle the prickings of conscience, he will have to learn the hard and often brutal way.

So let us not condemn others too quickly. Except for help along the way, or other factors not easily seen, any one might find himself heading toward Skid Row, for there are no brakes against a man's willful corruption of his divine quality of free will excepting those which he himself applies. Most individuals, whatever the tragedy of their present life, have deeply rooted within, seeded there by past experiences, untapped resources of strength and nobility; and once the will is quickened to turn in the upward direction, there are no heights so great that the basest man cannot, if he will, achieve.

Question — It surely looked as if the scales had been weighted against some of those people, as though God really had predetermined for them a course of evil. You don't believe that, do you?

Comment — I certainly do not. It may look that way, viewed from the closed circle of a one-life experience; but don't forget the continuity of consciousness that spans both birth and death. I realize how difficult it is for us who have been schooled to think of one short term on earth to welcome this idea of the rebirth of the soul again and again. I am not asking you to accept this idea, but only to consider it well before you cast it out.

The pattern of growth is not a hit-and-miss affair, but is the inevitable effect of the initial drive in the seed of godhood that is at the heart of every creature within the universe. Therefore the scales could not possibly be weighted against man. On the contrary, if they were weighted at all, it would be in his favor, for the pressure of the evolutionary current is ever forward, with the entire life-wave of humanity being slowly but surely carried along in its stream. There is nothing static in nature — either we go forward, or we go backward, and that is where the challenge comes in. In the kingdoms below man, the urge is ever upward toward the human kingdom, and growth there is automatic and without self-conscious direction. But in the human kingdom we must

decide which way we want to grow — for it is possible to
go downward, and way down; it is equally possible to make
great strides forward insofar as the quality of our consciousness is concerned.

After all, it is consciousness and what we do with it that
is the core of our problem. We have today a certain horizon
of consciousness that represents the sum total of what we
are, which horizon is for us at this moment a Ring-pass-not,
beyond which we cannot go. But the Father within is pushing and prodding us all the time, however unaware we may
be of his attentions, to expand that horizon and go beyond
our Ring-pass-not toward a more distant goal of understanding and wisdom. In the process of growth we make errors,
naturally, but we learn in time what is right and what is
wrong; and if the current of our aspiration is flowing toward
the light, that is all that is required. Either we go forward
with the life-wave of humanity toward our goal; or, if we
prefer, we can deliberately go downwards and break our
link with divinity — but this happens so very rarely that we
can discount it for the general run of mankind.

It is impossible for us to stay exactly on the same level of
consciousness, because every moment of the day we are
moving, hopefully, toward a greater field of vision and experience, and with each forward step we find a new Ring-
pass-not. When the moment of death comes, the quality of a
man's innermost thoughts through his lifetime will reveal him
to be either a weaker or a stronger character.

Question — Would you explain where the Devil fits into
your scheme? This isn't merely a hypothetical question, it's
a very real one for me right now. You see, my father was for

many years a minister, and quite broadminded I used to think; and he's a grand person too. But with the development of nuclear weapons, he has become quite rabid. He is convinced that it's all the work of the Devil. Nothing I say will change his mind. What do you think?

Comment — I can appreciate your problem, because it goes to the very heart of a man's inmost beliefs. Let me say first that I sympathize deeply with the horror your father feels at the use of nature's secrets for destructive purposes. Yet I for one cannot consider the birth and growth and present rapid development of nuclear physics as the work of the Devil — if there is one — or of any of his hosts of darkness. The usage of power for evil is always a devilish and fiendish thing — but it is not the work of Satan.

There is a big difference here. It may appear trivial, but it goes right to the core of the theological problem of good and evil: good as the manifestation of God, and evil as that of the Devil. To me there is no devil who willfully leads human beings into ways of evil; nor is there any personal God who as willfully leads human beings into paths of rectitude. However, good and evil, just as heat and cold, day and night, and all other bipolar manifestations, are always with us. But they are relative conditions of living beings, and not inherent entities in themselves. Therefore good and evil in human relationships are seen as relative states of consciousness. Good, we can say, represents that which is in harmony with the upward trend of progress; evil, that which tends to retrogress, to distort and upset the natural equilibrium. What seems good to some aborigines in Australia and Africa may seem frightfully evil to us — and, perhaps, vice versa!

Question — If, as you say, there is no Devil, do you think God allowed man to discover the secret of the atom?

Comment — I don't believe God had anything to do with our discovery of the atom, nor that God would stop us from exploiting its use. It will be man himself who will put the brakes on its destructive use. Also I believe so firmly in the law of cause and effect, that to me the discoveries of nuclear physics are all part of the greater opportunities that we as a race have earned. I think we need have no fear that headlong destruction will eventuate.

Question — Then you believe that man will go only so far, that he won't deliberately commit race suicide? You said earlier that if someone really wanted to go wrong and followed that way long enough, he would eventually go down and perhaps even break contact. Why wouldn't the same thing happen to humanity which, after all, is just a couple of billion human beings all together?

Comment — It could very easily, if there were sufficient desire in enough human beings to follow the path of destruction and evil. But I am as sure today, as I am sure of anything in this world, that the balance is strongly on the side of right. Why do I say this? Take a cross section of any city, community, nation or group of nations. You will find outstanding examples of the best and finest in human qualities, as well as the very worst; but alongside these will be the vast number of men and women whom no one ever knows by name but who, literally, are the "salt of the earth." In their simple way they are exemplifying qualities of courage, dedication to their particular duties, however humble and seemingly unimportant, and a natural under-standing of their neighbor. All of which is weighed in the balance of destiny, as accurately as are the more brilliant virtues and qualities of character displayed by prominent men. That the scales are likewise heavy with inertia, selfish-ness and greed there can be little doubt.

Viewed in perspective, I am convinced that history will look back on this age as one of the most perilous, yes, but also the most remarkable for spiritual as well as material advancement. For the discovery of nuclear fission has focalized an intensive and direct inquiry into essential values. This in itself, plus the prevalence of a common danger, is bringing about a subtle yet tangible consciousness of our oneness as humanity.

Question — I'm with you all the way there, and I guess most young people are. But there's another angle my father takes up. He says not only is this atomic age the work of the Devil, but it proves that we're all "born in sin." But I think this is a pernicious idea. Would you talk a little about this concept?

Comment — This is no criticism of the individual who may believe sincerely that man is born in sin, but I cannot agree with it any more than you do.

Let's take the first three chapters of *Genesis*, and see how unsatisfying they are if taken literally, but if understood as an allegory of the birth of man how truly meaningful they become. After creating the heavens and the earth in the first chapter, it came time for God, or the Elohim — literally 'gods' in Hebrew — to fashion man. So in the second chap-ter Adam was created out of the dust of the earth, and then the Elohim breathed into him "the breath of life; and man became a living soul." Then a garden was planted in Eden, in the center of which was placed the tree of knowledge of good and evil. After all the animals were formed, the Lord God realized that Adam had no companion, so he caused him to fall into a deep sleep and he took out a 'rib' and formed woman. Thus we have Adam and Eve now, in the garden of Eden, naked and unashamed, and warned not to eat of the *tree of knowledge.*

Now the third chapter: here a serpent appears and entices them to eat of the forbidden tree, for they "shall not surely die," but "shall be as gods, knowing good and evil." Eve listens, and sees that not only is it good to eat, and a lovely thing to look at, but a tree "to make one wise"; so she decides to try a piece of the fruit and shares it then with Adam. We read further of the terrible curse the Lord God put upon Eve for beguiling Adam, and that there would be sorrow and labor and strife through all the days. Now listen to the final part of chapter three concerning the *tree of life:* "And the Lord God said, Behold, the man is become as one of us, to know good and evil: and now, lest he put forth his hand, and take also of the tree of life, and eat, and live forever" . . . Therefore, Adam and Eve were cast out of the garden and the Lord God put cherubims and a flaming sword at the entrance to guard the *tree of life* from man.

That in essence was the Hebrew way of stating the genesis of our evolutionary growth from a state similar to the innocence and irresponsibility of the animals, to a self-conscious recognition of our humanhood. Originally androgynous, that is, containing the potency of both male and female, Adam entered a "deep sleep" during which the

Elohim removed one of his ribs — note in Hebrew the word also means "side"— which brought about the natural division of the sexes into two, and infant humanity wakened then as fully sexed men and women. With the tasting of the forbidden fruit came awareness of their "nakedness" or responsibility, and a desire then to "sew fig leaves"— to do something about their new-won knowledge.

Moreover, the serpent in almost every land was not originally a symbol of cunning or deception, but rather of wisdom and a bringer of light and understanding. If we consider the serpent of *Genesis* in the role of a "Lightbringer," which is what Lucifer means, we can see how amazingly different will be our whole concept of man's origin.

Question — Then how did we ever get this idea of being "born in sin"?

Comment — That is one of the destructive effects of literalizing the supposed Word of God — of taking a truth and making a dogma out of your understanding of it, which understanding might be completely wrong. You see, when Adam and Eve, representing infant humanity, were cast out of Paradise, they literally did "fall" from their former state of peace and blissful unconsciousness into one of struggle and turmoil, and the confusion of choosing between good and evil. However, Adam's so-called Fall from Grace was not a fall backward but truly a fall forward into expanded experience. Man was "born in matter," but not in "sin"; while he is "cursed" to toil and suffer, yet with the pain and struggle of every birth there comes always the beauty and triumph of creation. That is the heritage left by the Fallen

Angel, who taking the form of a serpent brought about that glorious bit of white magic, quickening latent mind into dynamic activity, and thus giving us our conscious connection with the breath of Divinity when the Elohim breathed into this lump of clay and made of man "a living soul."

Question — I have a question about God's will again. What is the best method to get into line with the will of God?

Comment — That is a beautiful question. Perhaps the most sublime rule of conduct is to be found in the Master's cry at Gethsemane: *Not my will, but Thine, be done.* Let not the will of the personal man take over, but, O my Father, work through me and bring thy divine will into function. If we can aspire toward the will of our Father, no matter how many times we fail or how seriously we may deviate from our inner ideals, we shall find that ultimately we will be doing not the will of the erring human self, but truly God's will, because it will be the will of our own inner divinity. God's will is not the same for you, or for me, or for anyone else; it is the divinity within each one of us, our own portion of God's essence, our own individual Father, which alone can make clear to us the will that we individually must follow.

You ask how best to get into line with our divine will? *Not my will, but the will of the Father, be done* — insofar as we are able to attune our prayers and our aspirations unto the Father and abide by his injunctions, we shall receive guidance in abundance. But, I repeat, no one can predefine for another what the will of the Father is. Each individual has the responsibility to determine that for himself. Nor are

95

his commands spelled out in so many words that we can hear. But they are there.

Thus you can see that man is his own monitor and guide, and he need have no fear because, though fashioned of the dust of the earth, he has the breath of the Elohim flowing through him, and as a "living soul" he can indeed "judge the angels."

Investment in Strength

THE STRUGGLE OF mankind to move from the darkness into the light has engaged the attention of generations of serious-minded citizens in every quarter of the globe. Century after century there have been individuals who have dared to storm the "gates of heaven," and infuse courage and a larger vision into the thinking of mankind. Side by side with these few, however, has been the dead weight of those who refuse to meet even halfway the responsibility of humanhood. Today the critical nature of decision is a universal challenge — no longer the privilege of the few, but the charge of all. But how to meet that challenge intelligently and wisely?

97

It is one thing to glimpse a vision of a more enlightened approach, quite another to implement it. The age-old virtues of charity, discrimination, courage and understanding take years, maybe millennia, to become a solid investment in character. Everywhere men are asking themselves: if the battle of light against darkness continues endlessly, what of the use of force in our human relationships? If we see nature using force in her kingdoms, how can we expect man not to use force to bring about his will?

In the process of growth, naturally there is struggle and a conflict of wills. But we can question whether nature ever *forces* her growth. There is a world of difference between the compulsion of force and the beneficent use of strength. In physical matters force undoubtedly works, for it takes only a few bulldozers and earth-movers to "remove a mountain." But in the higher levels of thinking and action, what do we invariably run into when force is applied? Opposition and more opposition, with force pitted against force, and no solution in view. Yes, in every human relationship we do indeed find force, plenty of it: the force of the human will trying to compel change, trying to bulldoze its way through mountains of opposition. But if there are mountains other than those of rock and earth, do they not require implements of the spirit rather than of matter?

The workings of nature are quiet, yet strong; and while man can take a flower in a hothouse and by the application of forced heat hasten its maturity, in doing so he speeds its death. We all remember the passage in *Matthew* where Jesus reminds his listeners that "from the days of John the Baptist until now the kingdom of heaven suffereth violence, and the violent take it by force." Should we infer that Jesus meant that we must literally take the kingdom of spiritual things by force? Looking into the original we find that this injunction can with equal accuracy be translated in this way: "The kingdom of the heavens is overpowered, and the strong (of mind) seize it." The verb "overpower," coming from the root *bia*, in ancient Greek usage signified not only "bodily strength or power," but also "strength of mind." So why not interpret the Master's admonition as "the kingdom of spiritual things must be taken by strength, and those of strong mind seize it."

The crisis of today is not new — it has been met countless times in ages past, but not in recorded history has there been so overwhelming a concern that our actions be enlightened. With every resource at our command, spiritual, mental and physical, it would seem that victory would be simple. Yet there remains ever the natural timidity of human nature to cast off the old and seize with strength the kingdom of the new. There still are Nicodemuses who stand aloof, by their own choice, outside the circle of active responsibility; and the rich young rulers who, feeling the pull of truth, yet prefer their bonds, the "riches" of their vested thought-vehicles, and thus deny themselves the privilege of joining the vanguard.

The hope of the world does not lie in doctrinal religion, in philosophic speculation, nor in scientific experiment. It lies where it has always been: in the courage and the vision of each succeeding generation to move with the tide of progress as it advances from one cycle to the next. We must look ever to the young in heart — not always the young in years, but the young in resilience of spirit — to chart new pathways of achievement so that the generations to follow may continue the upward progress of the race.

The youth of today are proving that there is a deep fund

99

of unselfishness in their natures, coupled with a desire to do something creative with their lives. Some of them, it is true, are encountering serious difficulty in making the adjustment to maturity, but these are an insignificant percentage compared to the pulsing life-wave of stronghearted, determined and highly intelligent young folk who are zealous in their endeavor to prepare themselves to meet the challenge of this century. Searching questions they ask, not the least of them centering on matters of birth and death, and their interrelationships as human units in the greater evolutionary plan. There is a self-reliance of spirit and of mind that no longer will accept the tired literalisms of religious dogma. The legacy of the "kingdom of heaven" is theirs — not for liquidation through force, but held in trust for the "strong of mind"— a legacy of freedom of thought, of action and, most important, a legacy of freedom in spiritual aspiration.

Psychic vs. Spiritual Development

QUESTION — The two of us here belong to a group of young people around the ages of sixteen to twenty-two. We meet regularly to discuss all kinds of questions, ranging from social and cultural matters to philosophy and religion, as we are interested in finding more satisfying answers than the usual religious sources have so far offered. We've looked into the ideas of reincarnation and karma, and even psychism, and should like to know your viewpoint on these things, especially on psychic development.

Comment — I emphatically do not encourage psychic development. It cannot be denied that man has such hidden powers and far more subtle forces within him, but they will come into active function naturally as the inner consciousness of the individual is able to utilize them properly. But this proper and wise use will not occur unless we first accent the fulfillment of our daily responsibilities.

Question — But when man has these inner powers, why should it be wrong to develop them?

Comment — Let me make this clear: while I myself definitely frown upon the forced development of extra-normal powers, I have no criticism of the individual member of any group who may believe otherwise. My criticism centers upon the misconception and misapplication of ancient spiritual principles. For millennia the sages have warned against an unnatural delving into the psychic, and have stressed the cultivation of the moral and spiritual as the chief line of endeavor. I speak only in principle, with no wish to influence you at all. But if we try to live what we can grasp of the truths that have been enunciated by all the world teachers, with no emphasis on psychic powers, then we will, by karma, attract to ourselves the very experiences that we require.

Spiritual enlightenment is something that is going on all the time, every hour of every day, and not just in organized gatherings or on Sundays or in special circumstances with particular ceremonials. Our main responsibility is to do our full duty — not only to our family, to our profession, but to our nation, our fellowmen, and not least to our higher self. After that, if we have any time and energy left, we can think about doing specific calisthenics in order to develop our spiritual muscles!

Question — Some of us believe in the rebirth of the soul, but what exactly is it that reincarnates?

Comment — What is the continuum of guidance in the experience of any human being? It must be something connected, either directly or indirectly, with the immortal self that takes birth from life to life. Some call it the reincarnating ego or element, that permanent part of us which has brought with it a portion of the assimilated experiences of the past, and which thus gives the impulse to action in any one lifetime, setting the stage for the soul to act and react. Where does the stage setting come from? The reincarnating ego does not consciously manufacture it. Karma sets the stage by drawing from that great reservoir of experience which each one of us has accumulated. Thus it allows our higher self to bring a personality to birth which will help round out and strengthen and increase the value and spiritual quality of the reincarnating ego. In the university of life the classroom is the family and environment in which we are born. And the teacher? Every one is teacher as well as pupil. All whom we contact in the course of growing up and living either will teach us something, or we have something that will give them what they need — it may be only a smile or a frown — a natural exchange that works infallibly, both ways, whether we are aware of it or not. It is our attitude toward the circumstances of life that makes our future, and gives us in the process the exact training that will allow our consciousness to expand into a broader understanding of our responsibilities.

Every great world religion has stressed in its own way the importance of cause and effect as a moral guide in the lives of earnest students. I say "earnest students" advisedly, and let me go a step further: every leader in spiritual thought has emphasized what I like to call the unfolding karmic script of our lives. Now you probably have studied something of man's threefold nature: the higher self, the middle self and the lower self. In our present stage of growth we are gaining firsthand experience in our middle self, the realm of the soul or the human ego. We can associate our thoughts and interests with the upper and find inspiration and guidance; or we can look toward our lower natures and become depressed and confused.

Question — Do you suggest any organized program for young people like ourselves?

Comment — My feeling is this: As every program of necessity encompasses individuals of differing character and karma, once you develop a set agenda of activity immediately you run the risk of trying to force everyone into the same mold of thought. You begin to crystallize something. This is wrong from the standpoint of the reincarnating ego that is striving so hard to work out its own pattern of growth. I know this sounds strange, and perhaps it is on the surface, but I am convinced of its fundamental soundness.

Among young people especially, at this point of the century cycle, there are egos who are entering earth life with a wider wave length of experience back of them than a formalized religious concept could possibly satisfy. They are seeking the living truth — not dogmas. The moment you try to fit one or more of those open-minded individuals into a prescribed plan of action, of thinking, of aspiration, he will revolt against such hemmed-in limitations.

Moreover, the climate of world thought will not be affected permanently by flash effects, by importunings. Too many organizations today work with that sort of thing, but their efforts, however sincere, peter out because serious-minded men and women are beginning to suspect that truth cannot be attained without individual sacrifice. There never has been, nor will there ever be short cuts to spiritual growth; and it would be a cardinal error to attempt to create such an impression.

Also let us not stumble into the pitfall so common in our highly specialized society, and think that if we deliberately organized a body of thoughts, or worked out a group of intricate formulas, just for the sake of achieving good results, our goal would be accomplished. We would find in the end that those very "good results" sought for would be nullified insofar as lasting benefit to humanity is concerned. Right here the ancient injunction to become unattached to the "fruits of action" is applicable. How often we act, even compassion- ately we think, and yet the undercurrent of our action is tinged with a selfish desire to *see* the good results, and to feel that *we* had a part in bringing them about. If we really wish to serve, then we should take no thought of results, for they are the concern of the Great Law whose operations are wiser and kindlier than man could devise. So let us shy away from formulas and incantations, or concentration on given thoughts for given ends. They lead us into byways that in most cases lure us from our main objective.

Question — This is very different from the manner of teaching as found in the churches, and even in education, where we are grooved to think along certain lines.

Comment — All of us must achieve understanding in our own way. Why should anyone who professes to have an interest in the welfare of his brothers try to make a 'canned' vehicle of thought into which to pour their spiritual energies?

It would be absurd. It is that very approach which has killed the work of the great teachers who have tried to inject into the thought-life of the world the pure stream of truth.

What happens when you and I exchange thoughts as we sit here together? Unconsciously to yourselves, you are pulling from me exactly what you need; and you in turn are helping me. That is the way karma works. It is not man-made; it is a law that flows from the Divine Intelligence. If we are acting within the moral structure of life, we shall know it and reap benefit; if we act against the laws of nature, we shall also know it, sooner or later, and will reap difficulty and suffering until we adjust our thinking and our attitudes. We cannot assess the karma of another, for we do not know into what areas of experience his higher self is leading him so that the proper values may be impressed on the soul. The wonderful part of it all is that our very mistakes are often our greatest teachers, for no one reaches a successful outcome except through conquest of failure. We need never be afraid therefore to make mistakes, for the light that will follow our learning from error will help us on the roadway of our future. Thus each one teaches himself; and, if the motive is sincere, when he slips, instead of falling with his face in the shadow and with darkness ahead, he falls uphill with his face toward the sun. That is occultism in its purest sense. The true occultist — not the false teacher of psychism or of the so-called 'occult sciences' which are fraught with peril — does not force teaching or instruction on anyone, but by the enlightening quality of example quietly points the way.

It is surprising how deeply these truths, which have been taught down the ages, are being activated today in the consciousness of our fellowmen. Thousands upon thousands are searching, just as you are. They are not interested in spiritual gymnastics; they want to know how to integrate their thinking with basic spiritual values in order better to meet the problems that are grinding into their consciousnesses. Certainly no demonstrations of psychic and extrasensory power will teach us. Only in the mill of life's discipline, at the end of each experience, will be found a measure of wisdom.

Question — In our group we have recently started inviting leaders in various branches of thought in order to compare their ideas with ours. But we have found that there are so many different brands of teaching. Do you think it is possible that some day all those who believe in higher things will work together in one organization?

Comment — I don't believe there ever will be a formal merging of outer organizations. Spiritual unity is an inner thing, and no amount of exoteric maneuvering will ever bring it about. However, in decades to come, perhaps in future centuries, it may be that a far greater number of individuals and societies will rediscover the common stream of spiritual principles and put them into practice in their lives. When this occurs, the outer framework of separate organizations will pass out of existence, and the inner unity of thought will consolidate the true values. Nothing could stop that, because these spiritual units in the vehicle of the heart of humanity would be working together, and the pulsebeat of truth would be circulating the lifeblood of evolutionary progress through the whole of mankind.

Question — But don't you think that all religions, all groups, have tried to do just that, only they have crystallized in different ways?

Comment — Unselfish endeavor, wherever expressed, will always contribute to the strengthening of the efforts of that small but potent nucleus whose goal is a wider exemplification of brotherhood among all men. In the course of each individual's doing his natural duty the peregrinations of goodness that occur will be unlimited. They do not stop at the two or three people with whom an exchange takes place, but continue on and on. Just as the ripples in a calm lake will widen into infinity, so will a sincere interchange of good works affect the entire body of mankind. It will be a genuine benefit, too, because it is a spontaneous expression of godhood and not a manufactured antidote for selfishness. Right action does spring from Divinity, from the wellspring of inspiration that spurs each of us on; and that is why the effect of a selfless act carries on ad infinitum.

Have you read the *Bhagavad-Gītā?*

Question — No, but we have heard of it. Would you advise our studying it?

Comment — I think you would profit by a careful perusal of the *Gītā*. There have been many translations into English and other modern languages. I myself prefer W. Q. Judge's Recension because, while not in poetry, in its prose form it has kept close to the original in spirit. It is a beautiful little book, profoundly esoteric beneath the surface of the exoteric story. The *Bhagavad-Gītā* itself is but one small episode from the great Indian epic, the *Mahābhārata*, and relates the adventures of two armies "drawn up in battle array," in the midst of which stands Arjuna who sees in the opposing army his "preceptors and friends" of old and refuses to fight. Krishna, standing for Arjuna's higher self, admonishes him to "arise" and face the foe of his former self. In the dialogue that follows, this principle among others of great value is enunciated by Krishna: out of hundreds of thousands, only one strives for perfection; and out of all those who do so strive, only one comes to know me as I am.

Now that same principle applies not only to the churches and all of these spiritual 'teachers,' but to the entire world of ideas: out of these there may be just one or two who have a relatively untrammeled perception. All the great religions in their first beginnings were expressions of truth. But alas, among the disciples who were most devoted to the 'new' thought, how many truly understood with the eyes of the soul? Only a portion was glimpsed; and when that portion was committed to writing it became fixed, and finally became a dogma. Their concepts may have been accurate from the vantage point of their own consciousness, but they were not necessarily truthful for everyone. Take any group of men, and go to any city or spot on this globe, and give them all identic views to look at, and then ask them to tell you what they saw. Each will give you a different story. So with truth — each of us perceives but a facet of a facet of truth.

Question — Would you say that people who try to develop their psychic powers are definitely going the wrong way?

Comment — How could we possibly say to someone else: "Your way is wrong; follow my way, because I know it is right." Only his inner motive can determine what is the right or the wrong path for him. But if anyone has as his prime objective the development of his psychic nature, then I would guess he was following a road that would eventually lead him into a blind alley.

Take mediumship, and the ability to see visions and thought-forms and to have power to read another's mind — all of these things have nothing to do with the spiritual nature. They are hindrances rather than helps, because they tend to entice the soul away from its goal. Why do I say this when there is such interest today in these extrasensory powers? As said, it is not because they do not exist; obviously, if they were but figments of the imagination, there would be little danger in them. But it is because of their very real existence that they pose one of the greatest challenges. You remember what the Master Jesus said: Seek ye first the kingdom of heaven, and all these things will be added unto you. This is what every world teacher has said: Seek *first* the path of spiritual enlightenment, the sunlight of the divinity within, rather than the moonlight of the psychic nature; then the rays of light from above will flow down through your entire nature, illuminating the daily affairs of your life. When this happens, "all these other things" will indeed be added unto us in their natural cycle. Then, and then only, will we be prepared to handle them wisely, and without hazard to ourselves and others.

Question — But that is rather a slow process. Many people don't like to wait for this, but prefer to hasten their growth.

Comment — Actually, the pursuit of psychic development, while seeming a faster and more colorful route, is a much longer avenue of experience, and eventually may lead into the dead end of psychic imbalance where, for the time at least, the soul finds itself out of alignment with the spiritual and physical poles of its nature. The *unnatural* forcing, by wrong meditation, breathing exercises, and other questionable practices *can* develop the psychic centers in man. But if this is done before the natural time for their flowering when understanding of their proper use would come, there is great danger that the soul's progress may be delayed for lifetimes.

If our motive is earnest and our aspiration is strong and impersonal in the direction of truth, we will eventually find that roadway that is essentially right for us, no matter how many wrong steps we may take in getting there. As Krishna says in the *Gītā:* "In whatever way men approach me, in that way do I assist them; whatever the path taken by mankind, that path is mine." In other words, in the largeness of time, regardless of what road we follow, ultimately the divinity within us is going to link up with its child. The task of the greatest as well as the least of the helpers of mankind is to quicken this process by being midwives to the souls of men. That was the mission of Socrates: to stimulate the soul qualities of the youth of Athens to fuller birth.

Spiritual unfoldment is one of the most moving experiences a man can have. However, if an individual is looking for some high-powered development, he will be sorely disillusioned. The only real drama is that of his own soul becoming wider and wider awake. When that happens, his vision of life and of all that is taking place in his inner nature as well as in the universe becomes intensely radiant with the fullness of spirit. That is drama at its highest.

As Little Children

In the Christian Scriptures we read that the Master Jesus said: "Except ye become as little children ye shall not enter into the kingdom of heaven." A statement so simple that for years and years we have failed to give it the attention it merits.

To whom was he speaking? To little children? To boys and girls? Not at all. He was speaking to adults, those who had problems both material and spiritual, and who had come to the Master for help. He knew their struggles, and he saw in their faces exactly what anyone may see today in the faces of men and women everywhere.

In times of crisis we become so caught up with the current

of the moment that we lose sight of the fact that the immedi-
ate situation is only one point in a long series of situations, the
culmination of years, perhaps lifetimes. Not recognizing that,
we lose perspective and cut ourselves off from the value of
those past experiences which, if understood, would help us
resolve our dilemma. So, blinded by confusion, we think we
are being imposed upon, not only by others but by life itself.
As a result, we blame everybody else — our neighbors, our
business associates, maybe even our family and close friends,
or the government, the world, anything — but ourselves. That
is what Jesus must have seen in the eyes of those to whom he
spoke those words. How clouded was their consciousness,
how many thick veils they had allowed to be built between
what they were when the Master saw them, and what they
were as children.

All of us have made our lives difficult beyond need. For
millennia we have prided ourselves on our learning, our
erudition, our understanding of truth. And yet the teachers
of the race have ever reminded mankind that the heart-
doctrine is to be preferred to the eye-doctrine: the learning
that is native to the heart, the intuition, the spiritual will of
man, rather than the learning that is purely intellectual and
motivated by the human will. Can't we realize that the
enigmas of life are solved not by mere reason, but by intuition; not by sentimentality, but by judgment?

Those of us who love children are astounded at the pure
intuition they express, amazed at times at their clear perception. Everyone knows that the hardest questions to answer
are those asked by the very little ones, who uncannily go right
to the core of the basic issues that often confound the world's
philosophers. And we will never satisfy our children by using

reason or sentiment alone; but how their eyes sparkle when we appeal to their innate intuition and judgment.

Why then did the Master urge his followers to become as little ones if they would attain the kingdom of heaven? Did he want them to return to childish pranks, and to act and think literally as children? Certainly not. He was appealing to that quality which was like unto the child. Let us look at ourselves today. What happens to us as we grow up? We go through school, perhaps university if we are fortunate. We begin to feel as though we are learning a great deal. But what do we do with that learning, whether it is scholastic or practical, religious or scientific? In many cases, we merely file it away in our minds for possible later use. This process goes on for years and, as a result, when we are confronted with real decisions, when we are plunged into the maelstrom of life's vicissitudes, what do we do? In our anxious state, and even after sober reflection, we attempt to pull out of our mental filing cabinet those things which we think will solve our problem, only to find that they do not solve it at all, either to the satisfaction of ourselves or to others who may be involved.

Now why? If we had stored the value of each experience in our heart, in the permanent part of our consciousness, then when we are brought face to face with serious matters, instead of trying to worry out the answers with our mind, we would discover that the heart, having taken over, would quite naturally lead us to the right solutions. The intuition then would have become our guide, and the mind its obedient servant, the implementor of its directives — not its master.

It might seem a most onerous task for those of us who are older and have made many mistakes, perhaps even grave ones, to become in a short time like a child. But that is not the case.

The Master Jesus knew it was not too hard or he would not have admonished the people of his day to do just that. And especially is it possible once a man has determined to give his life in service.

Let us ask ourselves this simple question: what is the foundation in the child's consciousness that allows his intuition and judgment to operate so beautifully? He is freshly arrived from another shore. And at his tender age he is unencumbered by an awareness of his past or his future, so that he has a truly virgin consciousness with which to prepare for the experiences ahead. He has come into life, as Wordsworth so graphically phrased it, "trailing clouds of glory."

What does the child bring with him most of all? It is trust — that genuine foundation upon which the spiritual growth of the world must be built. What human being who has any love in his heart cannot recognize that implicit trust in the eyes of a child who newly looks upon a world and his parents as greater than himself, to whom he can always turn? But as he goes through life, he finds less and less trust in the hearts of those with whom he must associate. As a result, he becomes confused, maybe even bitter.

To become as little children! There is a simple way of doing this which has been the same all down the ages: Man, know thyself! That injunction was not new to those who worshiped at the temple of Apollo, or who listened for and believed in the oracles of ancient Greece. It is timeless, as potent today as when first enunciated. The only way we can know ourselves is to search our consciousness. If we can do this honestly, we will stop blaming others for our trials. But we are so cluttered up with our filing system of mental facts, which we are so fond of, that we cannot break through to our hearts where intuition and help reside. Once we determine to face ourselves and assume the full responsibility of our circumstances, then the gods stoop down to help, at unexpected times, through unexpected persons, and in unexpected ways. This is an inviolable law and offers the foundation in fact of the famous expression of Hercules to the wagoner: "Put your shoulder to the wheel; the gods help those who help themselves." Until we become as little children we shall never attain that state of consciousness where we feel the full value and help of the spiritual forces that protect mankind.

Shortly before Christmas a letter was received from a ten-year-old girl, asking some questions which seemed best to answer by talking directly with her.

Expanding Horizons of Youth

YOU TELL ME NOW, in your own words and in your own way, just what you would like me to talk about.

Question — Well, Mother said something about the four special seasons. I'd like to find out about that.

Comment — The four sacred seasons? Well now, for centuries the beginning period of each season was considered sacred because the sun at that time, in relation to the earth, is at a definite point of changing from one position to another. For instance, about March 21st we have what is called the spring equinox, and in the fall about September 21st there is the autumnal equinox. The word means "equal night" because then the days and nights are equal in length, with as much daylight as there is darkness.

When we move from spring to summer, about June 21st, we have the longest day and the shortest night when the sun is farthest north in the northern hemisphere. At this period, midsummer, the sun appears to remain stationary for a day or so before beginning its journey south again. That is why we call it the solstice, the word meaning the "sun standing still." Now we are at the end of December when autumn becomes winter and have just passed the shortest day of the year and the longest night on or around December 21st. This is the winter solstice because the sun having reached its farthest point south seems again to "stand still" before it starts north once more.

So you see, the two equinoxes and the two solstices are the four points of the year when the ancients recognized that the whole world feels something different, and so they called them sacred seasons. You might wonder, what makes those periods sacred? Is it just because the sun happens to be north or south or on the equator?

In ages past, because the earth is part of the solar system — and this goes for the other planets also — many peoples knew that the earth gets its life from the sun. That is why they spoke of him as Father Sun, for without the sun nothing would live. Scientists today are saying the same thing, only using scientific terms, for they tell us that most of the vitality and energy from outer space comes to the earth through the sun.

Let me give you an example: you have to plant seeds during certain months of the year so that they will have a chance, during the longer days, for the sun to help them come out of the ground and bring forth the fruit and the harvest. That may not seem too important here but it is connected, for the ancients felt that at the change of the seasons a certain quality of solar energy comes in that affects the whole constitution of man. Especially at Christmas and the New Year a new, fresh life-force radiates from Father Sun into the world, and man, because he is the highest developed being on the earth, can consciously take advantage of this and help himself grow.

All of this taken together is very sacred. You see, we are completely dependent upon the sun; and the more we understand about the life-currents that flow to the earth — remembering that the ancients believed the sun to be a divine being at its heart just as we are, only much greater — the more we can try to live our lives in such a way that we will naturally benefit ourselves and those around us by taking advantage of the sun's special help at these seasons.

Now your letter mentioned your Jewish friend. Yes, they too have their own holy days, such as Rosh Hashana which is their New Year, and Hanukkah, and the Passover, and various other ones — just as we have ours at Christmas and Easter, and so forth. As we study other religions, we find there are many traditions and legends among the different peoples of the world which are connected with what takes place at these sacred periods of the year.

Take the story of Jesus: we have virtually the same story in every religion, about how a babe was born at Christmas time, which means that at the winter solstice there was the birth of a Savior. Whether the Savior was actually born on that exact day is unimportant; the fact remains that the New Testament did portray symbolically that a new virgin life-force came through for mankind at that period of the year, and coinciding with the turning of the sun northward again it has its own particular significance.

Then comes Easter after the spring equinox, which is the time when the story says they nailed Jesus to the cross. That is also symbolical. In those days, as you will learn when you study history, they used to punish criminals by nailing them on a cross and leaving them to die. So the ones who are supposed to have written the gospels used the crucifixion as a symbol. However, many people today really believe that the Master Jesus was physically crucified. But in the mystery legends of antiquity, we are told that we must begin to crucify ourselves — that is, get rid of some of the lower elements in our characters and in our own lives.

In the autumn we have the harvest, the time when the farmers in the fields gather their crops. A similar thing happens with us. We have the opportunity each year, if we have done our work in life satisfactorily up to the harvest period, to get the benefits of the good that we have accomplished. Just as the seed brings forth the fruit, so we will have produced the fruit of our own worthwhile efforts — maybe nothing tangible or objective, like money or food, but there will be something of spiritual value. Then, when the winter solstice comes around, we have the birth of a new year all over again.

That is very simply stated, and only in part, as I cannot go into a lot of related thoughts all at once. I don't want to burden you. But now why don't you tell me if there are any other aspects that you want me to talk about, and I will try to explain them so that this whole picture will become clearer for you.

Question — Another thing I wanted to know was this. I'll use as an example the Jewish people. Their religion is in Israel. Now is there any certain place where these ancient teachings you mentioned got started, or was it just all over?

Comment — At different eras in the history of our world, these great truths flourished in various centers all over the globe — at one time flowering in India and China, at other times in Egypt, Persia and Greece, in ancient America, in Britain and Northern Europe. This has been going on for a very long time because the age of the earth and of man is far, far greater than a few thousand years. The Christians used to believe that the earth was only some 6,000 years old, and that when the Bible said it was created in six days it meant "days" as we understand them. Of course, the ancient Hebrews did not think that, for they knew that their sacred books were always written in symbols which had to be understood properly. And, as you know, science has now proven that the earth is millions and millions of years old, and that the age of man is also many millions of years. So you can see that we as human beings have had a very long experience on our globe.

Sometimes there were civilizations which were very spiritual, and at other times there were those which lost touch with these noble ideas and became very material. But whenever mankind as a whole was in need of more understanding and help, a great teacher would come, at the right time, to explain once more the age-old truths. And these teachings were always the same in principle.

Sadly enough, human nature being what it is, the followers of these great teachers again and again made a religion out of each new inspiration. For example, not long after the Buddha died, the Buddhists made a formal religion out of his teachings; the Moslems did the same thing with the message of Mohammed; the Jewish people made set religious practices and rituals out of the inspiring example of Moses, and Christians have made a formal creed out of the beautiful teachings of Jesus. Now then, where did these ancient truths originate? We can only say, "all over the world" — in a different place each time. Does that help at all?

Question — Yes, very much.

Comment — You see, the great problem with religion of any kind is this: when you hear something from which you get a new understanding you begin to say, "this is it," and pretty soon you close your mind to a further glimpse of truth. That is an unfortunate thing because nothing throughout the universe remains forever the same. Everything is constantly growing, becoming better, man included. But when the followers of any faith keep on clinging to their particular view of truth, after a while it loses its vitality; it loses its living inspiration and therefore its helpfulness. So sooner or later, another teacher has to come in order to present the same "god-wisdom" in a fresh form.

Question — I am certainly glad that I feel the way I do about all these things, because I did attend church when I was quite small — well, six or five — and they kept telling me all those terrible things, that if I wasn't good, then when I died I would go to all this fire and everything. I was just real scared. I didn't believe it, you know, really . . .

Comment — That's the difficulty. It is the *wrong* interpretation of what the great teachers have said all down the centuries that has caused more trouble in the world and more fear in people's lives than any other thing. From my own studies I have come to believe that hell and heaven are states of mind, states of consciousness. There is no place where you go and are thrown into fire and brimstone and burn up, as they say. And there is no heaven as a place, with streets of gold, where you stay for all of eternity — who would want to be always walking up and down the streets of gold!

Question — I should think if I had to be up there forever and ever and ever, well, I would be extremely bored.

Comment — Of course you would, and everybody else would. But you know that those ancients we spoke of believed in and accepted the doctrine of reincarnation. In fact, there are very many young people today who feel sure they have lived before and that they will live again, and that they are here now on this earth in order to learn more and more. That is where a study of the older teachings comes in, because they give us the basis of our existence: why we are all living today and what we are to do about it, and where we go when we die. Not to a place called heaven or hell, but we do have a rest period during which we can get the benefit of all that we have learned during life. And then, we are told, with each return to earth we have the chance to go a little bit higher in the school of life. The more experience we have, the wiser we become and the better we can make our character, so that ultimately we too will be helpers of humanity, helping those who need help.

Question — Speaking of reincarnation, I had an experience last year when I was in fourth grade. My school teacher — I forget now the subject she started on — told us that some people believe in reincarnation. But she had it all wrong, because she said they believe that when you die you come back to earth in animal form, you know, or like a ghost or something. She said that. She had it all wrong.

Comment — Yes, I think that is wrong because, in the evolutionary growth of all living things, once we become a human being we cannot go backwards. We will always be a human being until we become something finer and better, like a god, or a divinity of some kind. Maybe a lower grade first, and then a higher and a still higher grade of divinity, until one day in the long, long distant future we might become like a sun, just as helpful as our sun, because, as I said earlier, the sun that we *see* is only the manifestation of a very highly developed spiritual entity, a supreme being, and the whole of the solar system is its vehicle of expression.

You will find, of course, there are many of these ideas that the children around you in school don't come in contact with. For instance, many of them would think you were crazy if you would talk about reincarnation. Your teacher certainly expressed only a partial view. We don't come back as animals, no; but we *do* come back as human beings and with a little more experience so that we can do better in each new life. But you, as the personality, will never come back again. You understand that, don't you?

Question — Oh, yes.

Comment — But what is now inside of you, that you know is there, and is using you as its temple, as its residence for this lifetime, will come back again. That part has lived before, and has had many personalities and many names. It is the immortal part, the real you, that comes for experience, that needed you this time — just as the real part of me needed my personality in order to do its work. Next life you might be a boy, you cannot tell; we have all been boys and girls. It is possible that we might even be the parent of our parents. In other words, they might be our children some day. We cannot know, but we don't need to worry about it. Karma, the good Law, takes care of all of this in a very positive way.

Question — Does a family stay together? I mean, could I be my father's grandmother or something?

Comment — A family may, but doesn't necessarily have to stay together. A lot depends on what lessons we came into this life to learn and how many of them we have learned when we pass on. But all those whom you come to love now you will meet again sometime, but maybe they won't always be a part of your family. We don't know. We cannot nor should we even try to cut life apart with scissors or make an analysis of it. One thing we can be sure of: each one of us comes into this world with a certain background experience from the past. We are born into the environment which will give us the circumstances, the problems and difficulties that we need to further our growth. We are drawn to the family which will give us the very quality of love and challenge that we have earned, and which will help us achieve our goals. We should not expect to be together with the same ones all the time. It may even be we will not have the same parents or relatives for one or two or possibly more lifetimes; but, later on, they may need some quality of experience that we have to share, and so we will be attracted to each other again.

127

Now you see what can happen: take your parents or mine, while their personalities and names will disappear, next time we may indeed have some contact with them, but not necessarily in a family relationship. It might be as close friends. There will be some kind of an attraction, maybe brief, maybe longer, for true love and friendship belong to the higher, the real part of us, and we will never lose any of the good that we have gained in the past.

Practically everybody, no matter how little he knows, wants to be a little better than he is today. It is only natural, because there is that spark of God, that light from the sun, that little bit of the Divine Intelligence in the heart of every living being, which is trying always to get us to become more and more like it. It is this that is the overseer, the guardian angel of each one of us . . . Go ahead, what were you going to say?

Question — There's a boy I play with sometimes. He always seems sort of scared about everything. If he does anything wrong, he is petrified about what might happen. And then my girl friend was talking with me. She was upset because she had not had a very happy time. She was afraid to do what she really wanted to do for fear she'd make a mistake, because this was her only chance. They think this is their only life.

Comment — That's wonderfully stated, and it is a pity that more young people do not have the bigger concept of what life is all about, instead of this narrow feeling of fear and being petrified that if they make a mistake or do anything wrong, this is going to be the end of everything for them. Don't go out of your way to do so, but when your

128

friends talk to you about these things, just say you don't believe in hell and fire or that you burn forever and ever. You believe that we have more chances in which to learn about life.

If we try to do the right thing we will get the right answers, but if we do the wrong thing, of course we will feel the reaction — just as our finger will burn when we stick it in the fire. If we are really sincere, we know inside when we have made a mistake, but once we realize it, we don't need to make the same mistake again. No, we make our own heaven and our own hell, and there is no one who can say truly that you or I will go to hell or to heaven because we did this or that.

The important need today is for us to try to eliminate this awful fear that has been instilled in us. I had it when I was young, but I think it is a terrible thing to teach a child to believe that way. Naturally, I was not satisfied with such a cruel view and I kept on asking questions and looking around until I found what I considered to be the answers, just as you are doing. You are fortunate that you have parents who are not narrow-minded, and that you have others with whom you can talk over these things.

Now is there anything else?

Question — Yes, I have another question. It's about other lives on other planets or some place, like Mars and Venus. That has always interested me.

Comment — Well, . . . let me put it this way. The good Law has brought us back to earth, where we will continue to be born time and time again until we have learned all that this planet has to offer. When we are finished here, then we will be born elsewhere, to learn all that is to be learned on a higher level of experience, call it a planet, if you want.

Question — What is so nice about it is that you know that you keep on going, instead of having *one* chance and then going some place and staying there forever and ever.

Comment — That is the beautiful thing about the truth and the wonderful thing about nature, and about our infinite possibilities for growth. And not only that. After we reach the point at which we are a sun, let us say, way off in the future, and we have done our task well and have experienced all that we can as a sun, even that is not the end, because from there we go on still further. We are told that the Divine Intelligence that is the real heart of our sun, and in a sense is the higher part of our solar system, imbodies in it only until the sun-being learns all that is to be learned as our sun. Then the solar entity has to go higher still — there is no end to growth — to become after many ages what some have called a Rāja-sun, meaning a "kingly sun," which is the sun over many suns.

Question — I like *that!*

Comment — Our solar system is not the only one in our galaxy or Milky Way; in fact, there are numerous suns, you see, attached to one Rāja-sun. And when our own sun has achieved all it can in its family of planets, it may become the sun of another, greater system, a more highly advanced one, until it becomes a Rāja-sun with many sun families as part of its constitution.

Question — It just keeps going on — our sun brings light

to the earth, and then there are other suns, higher than this one, that . . .

Comment — . . . bring life to our sun. That's right, that's how it goes, ad infinitum. It is an endless chain of sharing the divine life-force with everything that is living in space.

Question — I understand a lot more now. And the Bible and God and Jesus — that sounds just like these old teachings, only put kind of in story form, like God giving life to the earth and giving life to people.

Comment — That's right. We can, of course, take all of the statements in the Bible literally; but if we did, then we would have to believe the world was made in six days of twenty-four hours each, and we would also think there is a heaven and a hell, all of which we feel is not correct. But when we interpret it spiritually, we read the stories in it as symbols of the real teachings about life, symbolic expressions of spiritual principles operating in nature, and then we get the true answers. As you come to study the Bible more, as well as the sacred writings of other peoples, which you will some day, you will understand better how to apply these principles.

There is no end to the possibilities and opportunities of growth, no end whatever. Space is infinite, so there is room for universes beyond universes and galaxies and still more galaxies. And all these universes and galaxies have their life periods and their rest periods, just as human beings. Our solar system will have a rest period some time when all of its life and consciousness will be withdrawn. Then it will be born again, and perhaps the Divine Intelligence behind the sun will imbody itself in a different aspect from the one we see now. That all depends. Now, the period when a sun is in life has been called a *manvantara*, which is the Sanskrit word for such a cycle of activity, while the rest period is called *pralaya*. When the solar system is born again, this will be another *manvantara* or life period, just as we have our lifetimes. In a limited way our days of activity and our nights of sleep are very similar. Somebody has said: Sleep is a little death, and death is a big sleep. And that is the way it is.

Question — Don't you think that when the Bible was written it was really meant to be read to get the idea? Of course some people read it literally, and then you get all these things that are hard to understand. I guess it depends on the person.

Comment — The great teachers themselves never wrote anything, and that is what makes it so difficult. Some people think that God wrote the Bible, but God did not write it. Take the Old Testament. Some great teacher expressed these teachings orally and then someone else wrote them down later; and the same thing is true with the New Testament. It was the disciples, or possibly even their followers, who wrote down what Jesus was supposed to have taught. So when the teachings are finally written, we have only *others'* interpretation or understanding of them which is not necessarily what the teacher really meant. Thus, when we study the scriptures of any religion, it is essential to try to get the spirit behind the words of what was said.

Every human being will one day realize that what he is *inside* is the important thing, and that the best answers are those we work out for ourselves. It was never intended that any creed or any person should stand between you and your Father within, between you and that divine spark of Intelligence, because that is sacred to you. Just so, you shouldn't believe anything I say unless it rings true to you and something inside of you says: "That is what I think." If it does not, then don't believe it.

I certainly appreciated your questions, and I hope that what I have said has been of some help. Perhaps we can get together again some time.

Conscience and Intuition

QUESTION — I have been trying to reconcile the idea that to really know a thing you have to experience it, with the problem of good and evil. None of us goes through life without making mistakes, and experience does seem to teach us faster than anything else. My question is this: why don't we go ahead and do all sorts of things so as to get the experience over with?

Comment — You mean, just disregard the principles of right and wrong, and give vent to every impulse in order to get experience? You would be surprised how many sincere persons develop such an attitude, particularly in the fields of inquiry which may be termed 'occult.' But it is a twisted concept, and against every decent instinct of man. While it is true that the broad standards of right and wrong often vary depending upon the customs and conditions of different peoples, the age-old principles of morality have always been and remain today the foundation of progress. If we lived only one life on earth, there might be some justification for this attitude. But when we consider the larger perspective of the soul's pilgrimage through a series of lifetimes, we realize that such rationalization could easily lead into avenues of conduct that are counter to the purpose of evolution.

For ages all of us have been exercising our free will and thus have set in motion all sorts of causes, some of which we have already encountered as effects, and others are still to be met. In any one life we shall be faced with the type of opportunities we need in order to build our character, and therefore we don't have to rush out and seek experience so that the soul can grow. We never have to make a situation to experience, never. The inner laws would be working inside out if that were the case. Everyone knows inherently the difference between right and wrong, between following a good impulse and an evil one. Nevertheless, because we are still very imperfect, the human part of us tends to justify our actions when we deviate from a sound basis of ethics.

In the old days our forebears found no difficulty in distinguishing between what was good and therefore of God, they said, and what was evil and therefore of the Devil. In some ways there was a healthy austerity in their stand, which we might well emulate *in principle*, for it brooked no compromise with what one knew to be wrong.

Today, however, through the impact of world-wide relationships and the more conscious participation in the suffering of others, we have come to realize that good and evil, while distinct and separate as end products, nevertheless blend so gradually the one into the other that we are at times hard put to say where evil stops and good begins, where falsehood ends and truth remains, where white is still white, and not a dismal gray. Our vision of basic issues has become blurred because we seem unable to fix a firm dividing line between what is right and what is wrong. Somehow the wide bridge of right principles seems to have so narrowed that man has all but lost his footing.

Often too we participate ignorantly in situations without any conscious recognition that we are doing wrong. It is only later, as we run into trouble, that we begin to recognize that we acted wrongly, or at least unwisely. Then if we are again faced with a similar situation, we can either profit by our past experience and act with a little more wisdom; or we can succumb to the tendency to act as we did before, even though we know better. If we do that, then the voice of conscience will go into action and say: "No, this is wrong." If we don't listen to it, but go ahead anyway, that is where the battle begins.

Question — Do you mean that your conscience won't work unless you've already experienced a thing before?

Comment — Our conscience cannot give a danger signal unless we have experienced something in the past that made us suffer and therefore left an impression of warning in the soul, which now the conscience is trying to recall to our waking consciousness. But right here is the difficulty: it is true that the soul must learn all the lessons this earth has to teach, but that doesn't mean we should deliberately follow

137

the impulses of the lower material self in order to evolve. To follow that procedure would be to ignore not only the voice of conscience but the divine spark that is trying so hard to awaken our spiritual intuitions.

Question — There might be circumstances where we would go through all kinds of things but learn very little from them. If we committed a serious mistake, wouldn't we sooner or later have to recognize it as such before we would get any conscience reaction?

Comment — If you didn't learn the lesson, your conscience would not be ready to warn you. Until we gain the knowledge and understanding that an experience calls for we don't really learn, nor will we have the benefit of guidance from the conscience reaction as you put it. Just going dumbly through an experience doesn't help very much. We have to react with some sort of recognition of what is good and what is bad: but that does not mean we should go after experiences just so our conscience will tell us in the future what not to do.

We have a large area in which to exercise our initiative in the natural affairs that life places before us. In the soul of each one of us is a vast reservoir of experience — all of which has created the potent atmosphere of plus and minus in which we now find ourselves, but which in the future can be all plus if we handle it properly. It is what we do with that load of responsibility now that will create, or fail to create, a stronger voice of conscience; or, if you like, a stronger link with our higher self. We learn when we have suffered hard enough to want to change the course of our thinking, and not go on in the same old way.

Question — Do we have to experience the same thing we did to someone else? If I kill a man, do I have to be killed in order to realize I did wrong and shouldn't kill?

Comment — I am glad you brought that up. It is true that we cannot do unto others a negative thing and not have it react upon ourselves. But that does not mean that the old Mosaic law of "an eye for an eye and a tooth for a tooth" always works out in that *literal* manner. The original intent of that maxim is sound and basically true, but we do not have to suffer the identic re-enactment of an experience. In other words, we may not have to have an eye taken out if we take out the eye of another, but the *quality* of the experience of losing an eye will be ours. Do you see the difference?

You kill "X," let us say, in anger, or with malicious intent. It does not mean that "X" is bound to kill you in some future life. However, you will have to endure the quality of agony that you caused him to suffer when you willfully took his life. You may now or in the future lose your life by accident or by the deliberate act of someone, but it need not be "X" who brings that about; it may even be a quite impersonal thing such as a tile falling on your head. If you are sincere and truly regret the act, then when the effect catches up with you, the reaction to the original cause will be felt, but not necessarily physically. The principle of cause and effect holds absolutely, but its expression may shift from the physical to the mental or other planes of consciousness. Nevertheless, each one of us must meet the full reaction of wrongdoing by undergoing the quality of suffering that we bring upon others. We all know that mental and psychological pain can be far more severe than physical pain; it may be too that the reaction to a former transgression may be absolved in a moment of intense suffering, or in a flash of recognition — which is rarely physical. Once the quality of past error is fully experienced, the impress on the consciousness is so deep that the voice of conscience would almost shout should you again be faced with a similar temptation.

Question — Are those who deliberately run after experiences, even when they know they are doing wrong, starting a chain-reaction that sooner or later will reflect back on them through suffering?

Comment — Those who deliberately choose to commit wrong know better. When they flout the warnings of their conscience they are compromising their own souls, and are making an entirely different kind of karma from the one who ignorantly participates in wrongdoing. They will, in time, suffer horribly in realization. The field of subtle temptations ranges anywhere from the simple white lie to murder perhaps, including every type of indulgence.

Question — But isn't it rather ticklish to attempt to judge any person, because how could you tell what motivated his actions, what was really the impulse behind them?

Comment — Certainly we should never judge the motive of another, nor can we evaluate his progress by our standards. That is where so much of our pain and heartache arises. We would have to put ourselves in the shoes of another before we could possibly know how we would walk his pathway. We do have the responsibility, however, to discriminate between right and wrong action, and it is quite possible to discern in degree the quality of thought that prompts an act. But we cannot know the inner motive of others, especially of one who may by strong aspiration have brought upon himself great outer obstacles which he is finding hard to surmount. You remember the warning of the old sage: "Don't shrink from the beggar's robe, lest it fall on your own shoulders" — the principle being that we all have karma to work out now and in the future, and we can never tell when the wheel of life may find us underneath instead of on top, or vice versa.

We grow slowly, and life is such that we attract what we need — not always what we want — all of which adds to the treasury of our permanent self. We are very old individuals, and our experience accumulates as we go; and the law of attraction and repulsion operates so accurately, with such perfect delicacy, that the *quality* of thoughts and feelings that we have in any lifetime will in the future bring to us exactly what the reincarnating ego requires to complete and extend its growth up the evolutionary ladder.

Put simply, when we follow a line of conduct that is not upright or on a level with our own inner standard, we are going backwards; and this a hundredfold if we attempt to fool ourselves into believing that we "need the experience" in order to evolve. We learn from failure, yes; and the experience of pain gives sensitivity and wisdom to the conscience. But we should have done with continued descent into materiality and be up and on with the cycle of progress toward spirituality.

Question — If we grow through suffering, wouldn't all of us have to go through some pretty rough times if we ever want to change belief into knowledge?

Comment — The opportunity to transform belief into knowledge need not mean suffering always, but could be something wonderful. To have the right attitude toward everything that comes to us *is* wonderful. That's why I keep hammering at the idea that there is no good or bad karma — it is all opportunity for the soul's expansion. What we today may think is a terrible karma, to somebody else may be just the opposite, because that person has the right inner attitude and sees the events of his life in perspective and therefore understands them.

It all ties into the statement of Krishna in the *Bhagavad-Gītā*: "And even those also who worship other gods with a firm faith in doing so, involuntarily worship me, too, albeit in ignorance." That doesn't mean that everyone must accept Krishna as his God. What it means is that we shall all ultimately find truth, the real universal truth. If we are sincere we shall attract in some lifetime the opportunity to confirm or deny our belief, and thus come nearer to the truth which is One — Krishna, Buddha, Allah or whatever term applies. Then belief will have become knowledge.

Question — Wouldn't this kind of thinking and acting have two goals? First, to attract experiences of the right quality; and second, to strengthen our ability to act according to what we may know, and not only believe? In other words, from crawling we really start to walk?

Comment — Yes, walking more strongly, more firmly on the true path, because we are utilizing what life has given us to know. By doing so we more potently attract that which will help us enlarge our beliefs and in time transform them into knowledge — all of which will leave its impress on our character. But keep in mind always the basic coloring that motive gives to our aspirations: if we are learning and searching for truth for ourselves alone, that is one thing; but if we are pursuing that search that we might be worthy members of the human race and thus able to share by example rather than merely by precept, then we will find "knowledge springing up spontaneously" within ourselves.

Question – The more you think about this, the more difficult it is to analyze where belief leaves off and knowledge starts. Perhaps what we think are mere beliefs might really be recalling knowledge?

Comment – Exactly, and you will remember how Plato speaks in his *Dialogues* of the soul's re-collecting or reminding itself of its former knowledge, his idea of 'reminiscence,' the re-calling of the higher knowledge that has been stored up in the character in previous lives. It is important to be alert to this process. It may be that your experiences will not give you the opportunity to confirm your belief before death; but nothing is lost, because you will automatically draw to you the very conditions and contacts that will extend your present knowledge.

For example, what started you in this life searching for the answers? Perhaps it was an article which sparked a totally new line of thought; or you contacted an individual who without conscious effort changed your destiny; or some revealing incident may have tapped your latent strength. So in the future, whatever the outer cause, gradually karma will crack the shell of inertia and give you more and more opportunity to catch up with your innate knowledge. None of us reaches maturity at a given period, and I do not mean physical maturity; I refer to that point in this life where we catch up with ourselves from the past, and start to become more consciously allied with our true self. This attraction comes about naturally so that what we are becomes revealed to us, and then not only are we more sensitive to the prickings of conscience, but our intuition, an aspect of our higher self, makes itself known, and undeniably so.

The knowledge that you brought with you will penetrate ultimately your brain-mind consciousness. If the knowledge is there and our aspiration has unlocked the door to it — provided we don't delude ourselves by our ambition to know more and more with our mental processes alone — then the intuition, the voice of a higher consciousness, will act as a working instrument together with the voice of conscience. Now our conscience never tells us what to do, any more than the daimon of Socrates told him what to do. Its job is to warn us when we step over the fine line of right thought and right action. The reason our intuition doesn't speak to us oftener is that we, with our anxiety to collect brain-mind facts, simply don't give it a chance. Yet that intuition will not fail to give us guidance when we allow it to have stronger reign in our lives.

There is nothing fantastic about it, for when we have our consciousness targeted in the right direction, with the right quality of thought, we catch that glimpse of eternity that enables the soul to follow its natural pattern of growth. Then as the line of recognition between belief and knowledge becomes ever more sharp, and our discriminating ability becomes more clear, we may attract just the type of experience that will impel us to pledge ourselves, wholly and completely, to the benefit of others.

The Plus and Minus of Regret

QUESTION — I have been doing quite a bit of reading lately, and in one book, *Letters That Have Helped Me* by W. Q. Judge, I ran across the statement: "Regret nothing." Frankly, that disturbed me, because I had always believed that the moment you realized you had done wrong you should regret it sincerely, and try to do better. What deterrent is there to hold a person from doing wrong if he isn't ever to regret?

Comment — Your confusion may come from isolating the two words "regret nothing" from the surrounding thoughts. This is a rather risky thing to do, because it often distorts the

145

original meaning. The essence of thought behind the phrase is probably this: don't waste precious time and energy in *useless* and *vain* regret.

Question — Well, I can see that. But the statement was simply "regret nothing" and that bothered me. I was thinking of small instances in everyday life. If I were to offend someone thoughtlessly, and then later realized I had, I would regret it and my impulse would be immediately to say: "I'm sorry, I was thoughtless." Somehow that would help to re-establish a feeling of harmony between us. But if we are to regret nothing, how will we ever let the other person know that we are sorry?

Comment — Let us not be too limited and literal in our application of this thought. Obviously in our daily relations with others we should follow the natural rules of courtesy and conduct. If we offend another, or are thoughtless, of course we should feel sorry and the first thing we should do, if we have the opportunity, is to say so and thereby attempt to amend any infraction of harmony. If we ignore the rules of common decency, and attempt to hide behind this axiom "Regret nothing," then we will be making a far graver mistake than the original careless act.

Do you have the book with you? Good. Let me read the full paragraph:

The Past! What is it? Nothing. Gone! Dismiss it. You are the past of yourself. Therefore it concerns you not as such. It only concerns you as you now are. In you, as now you exist, lies *all* the past. So follow the Hindu maxim: "Regret nothing; never be sorry; and cut all doubts with the sword of spiritual knowledge." Regret is productive only of error. I care not what I *was*, or what any one *was*. I only look for what I am each moment. For as each moment is and at once is not, it must follow that if we think of the past we forget the present, and while we forget, the moments fly by us, making more past. Then regret nothing, not even the greatest follies of your life, for they are gone, and you are to work in the present which is both past and future at once. So then, with that absolute knowledge that all your limitations are due to Karma, past or in this life, and with a firm reliance ever now upon Karma as the only judge, who will be good or bad as you make it yourself, you can stand anything that may happen and feel serene despite the occasional despondencies which all feel, but which the light of Truth always dispels.

Let me try to explain this from the standpoint of man's nature: as soon as the human soul feels regret for some transgression, that feeling is impressed upon the consciousness and begins from that moment on to strengthen and build up the conscience. Thus regret is a necessary stage, but it is only a *stage*. That former wrong act may not have been done in this life at all, for the time element is the least important factor. It is the *quality* of our action which was impressed with indelible sureness upon our soul, and it is that which warns us now, through the voice of conscience, when we tend to follow a course of thinking or action that we should have outgrown.

Question — Don't we have to feel regret in order for our conscience to work?

Comment — Again let us not take any statement or rule of conduct too literally and miss thereby the spirit of the thought. If we judge everything we read solely by the words used or apply them out of context, we are being as dogmatic as the most orthodox die-hard. "The letter killeth, but the spirit quickeneth and giveth life." Naturally we must feel something, we must experience a reaction to wrong action done, else how would we learn? Once this reaction is registered, then is the time to apply the "regret nothing" rule, because regret from that point on, harping on our mistakes, feeling sorry for ourselves on account of the errors we have made, will yield but more sorrow. Learn the lesson; then go ahead, using our energy to strengthen other aspects of our nature, and to imbed the right attitudes of thought and feeling into our consciousness so that we build rather than destroy.

In order to better understand this concept of non-regret we must view it from the standpoint of many lifetimes. In fact, we should properly stretch our perspective to take in the whole gamut of our experiences from the Garden of Eden period on — from the moment we became individual men and women, with self-consciousness and the free will to choose what to do with our newly acquired knowledge of good and evil.

Question — Well, if you're going back to the time of the Garden of Eden — how many thousands or millions of years is it? — I guess we've done all sorts of things we wish we hadn't! Do you suppose we felt regret, way back there?

Comment — As soon as we recognized we were doing wrong, hopefully our conscience needled us sufficiently to make us want to change. But probably most of us have repeated the same mistakes many times. Yet those errors once recognized, far from holding us back, became stepping-stones to future success. The physical act is not half as important as the quality of consciousness that brings it into being. Change the quality of our thinking and feeling, and the quality of our acts will inevitably follow suit.

Question — Supposing you do a really bad thing, and don't realize how serious it is at the time; but later you wake up with a shock and feel dreadful. Can you erase that deed by sincere repentance? Is there such a thing as being "forgiven our sins"? I mean, if you are in dead earnest and want awfully to undo the wrong done, can you erase the error by remorse?

Comment — Once an action is done, it cannot be undone — all the tears and lamentations and repentance in the world will not make the slightest difference in life's ledger of debits and credits. However much we may wake up later, we cannot undo the past. What is done is done, and the action, whatever its quality, will inevitably, as day follows night, have its corresponding reaction. There is nothing cruel or arbitrary in this. It is simply that nature's law is inexorably just and — viewed in the light of the soul's growth — is immeasurably compassionate. For it is by the pain of reaction that we grow, and grow strong inwardly, and thus are able more fully to express the quality of the divine spark that is at the heart of each one of us.

So let us not be discouraged: the very recognition, however late in the day it may come, will work its magic of transmutation in our character. When the time comes for us to face the reaction of our error, we will have so strengthened the fiber of our nature that we can meet whatever the effects may be with courage and a new vision.

Question — Can we ever get rid of the "ball and chain" of karma? If I do something wrong and regret it later, will it return upon me again and again, cause and effect, cause and effect, with each effect making a new cause, enchaining me in its effect, so that I can never escape?

Comment — That is a totally erroneous concept. This "law of Compensation," as Emerson termed it, the law of balance, is not a merciless round of cause and effect with no hope of escape from the "Wheel of Existence," as the Hindus call it. True, it is like a wheel in that causes set in motion are bound, just as the wheel rotates, to return upon us as effects. But life is not a closed circle — the evolutionary pattern is spiral, and at each revolution there is opportunity to move either upward or downward on that spiral.

Once an action has worked round to its corresponding reaction, once a cause has manifested its effect, that originating cause is dead — it ceases to be, unless by an improper attitude toward its effect *we give it new life* and force it to become a new cause for future reaction upon us. It all depends on how we meet the effects. That is what many do not realize, because they have the idea so firmly fixed that since every cause has its effect, that very effect has a life of its own apart from what we give it by our reactions to it. The tragedy is that too many of us allow this to happen because we are not willing to meet our daily karma head on as it comes. Thus by our very shilly-shallying we enmesh ourselves further, revitalizing those effects so that in truth they do indeed generate future causes, which again we will have to meet as effects until the lesson of the particular experience is learned. It is our attitude towards the effects of our karma that will generate new causes for new effects — nothing else.

It behooves us therefore to avoid 'over-regretting' and

cut the doubts of our true strength with the sword of spiritual knowledge. The past is gone; the present *is;* and since the future is the fruit of our present actions it is what we do *now* that is most important. We can see how detrimental to the soul it is to spend energy and time in vain and unfruitful regret; for instead of allying our forces with the side of growth, we delay our progress, doing no good either to ourselves or to others. Once the recognition of wrong is clear, and the correct route seen, then let us turn our face to the sun, and march onward into the future. In this way we will have strength and perhaps a little wisdom to meet the effects of the countless causes we have set in motion in the past.

Question — I don't suppose we have made only bad karma. Haven't we made some good karma too?

Comment — Of course we have. Man's continued existence through the eons is in itself testimony of his divinity, and of the receptivity of the soul to the divine promptings. But karma is neither good nor bad — it is strictly impersonal, the impersonal working of the law of balance, which manifests as attraction and repulsion, as love and hate and cause and effect. Like the sun or the rain, it shines or falls upon the just and the unjust, warming and nourishing the soul in its upward climb. The meeting of the effects of our past thinking and feeling, acting and resolving, is therefore neither good nor bad; it is all *opportunity*, a wondrous opportunity for experience and growth.

Question — I am still thinking about that phrase: regret nothing. Do you suppose we are being warned not to regret in order to ward off the danger of becoming so immersed in regretting things that have happened that we become blinded to the very cause of our difficulty?

Comment — Everything is double-edged, and from one angle the fact that we do feel regret shows where our allegiance is, for unless we felt concerned over our mistakes we certainly wouldn't be on the higher road. It is the staying down in the mire of regret that is warned against, for an unhealthy repentance is contrary to nature's purpose. Moreover, there is a type of remorse which is nothing other than self-pity, when one feels so terribly about a mistake that it becomes an obsession. This is highly dangerous, because such a state of depression can become a habit and, if not checked, lead to that pernicious type of self-indulgence which is the first step toward mental unbalance.

That is one reason we shouldn't waste vital spiritual energy in remaining regretful. All of us are liable constantly to error, in judgment and even in motive. But that is nothing to be alarmed about. It is all part of evolution. If we had never made a mistake, if we had never had to face and conquer temptation, how strong would we be? When we do wrong, nature compassionately reacts and we suffer accordingly. "Even as gold must be tried in the fire, so must the heart be tried by pain."

Question — May I ask a question here? It is very simple, but it is important to me. How do we learn? Actually to put the principles of ethics into practice seems to be so difficult. How can we be sure we aren't fooling ourselves and thinking we're spiritual when we may really be quite self-centered?

Comment — That's a very practical question. Spiritual

attainment comes about as naturally as the night becomes the dawn. It is the inevitable outcome of right thinking and right action, not forced by rigid unnatural methods, but the result of the faithful performance of our one-pointed duty. The open sesame to true progress is *living* — not in one or two dramatic moments, but throughout twenty-four hours of each day. We learn both from our successes and our failures. The failures often prove our greatest blessings, because they shock us out of our complacency. So never regret the failures, for they burn the truth deep into the soul.

It is the interplay of action and reaction, of the natural working of the law of balance from lifetime to lifetime that makes us what we are today. We are now the sum total of all of our past, and the immortal part of us, the reincarnating element, is today attempting to utilize the very circumstances of our associations and environment to help us learn the lessons we need. The so-called good karma is often far more difficult to handle, strange as that may seem, than the so-called bad karma. When we have unpleasant circumstances to face we naturally check up on ourselves to see wherein we might have failed, or where our character might need a bit of strengthening; and the more painful the karma, the more sharply defined will be that quality which needs straightening out. If we meet it with fortitude and intelligence, real progress can be made. But when the karma is pleasant, too often we take it for granted and let down our guard, tending to slide both in our attitudes and aspirations. No wonder the Master Jesus remarked to his disciples: "It is easier for a camel to go through the eye of a needle, than for a rich man to enter into the kingdom of God." And he wasn't pointing only to the riches of this earth — he was trying to alert us to the need for vigilance all along the strait and narrow path.

That is why we are here on earth so that hopefully we may learn how to read the signposts of the unfolding script of our daily experiences and see what the higher self is pointing out for us to accomplish. As we succeed, the divinity at the core of our being will find opportunity to bloom more fully in our lives and we shall the better share with our fellowmen that which we have rightfully earned.

Coal or Diamond?

As a Pennsylvania boy, I was proud that my home state could boast of some of the biggest forests the earth had ever known. It didn't matter that they had disappeared; the fact that they were once there was pretty wonderful to me. Of course, they flourished millions of years ago, in some Carboniferous Age, but it was a thrill to realize that the carbon dioxide which those trees had absorbed so long ago had, under the pressure of soil and rock and time, gradually been metamorphosed into coal.

It seemed obvious to me even then that nothing really dies. Things changed form, but the energy that made them live simply went somewhere else. For all I knew, the force that had once caused the sap to flow through those pines might still be around, perhaps making our present forests green while underground their ancestral trunks, now transformed, had become a means of livelihood for thousands. Miners for generations had been digging out the coal, oil drillers pumping crude petroleum from shale beds, geologists had painstakingly gathered plant and animal fossils, while along the rivers and valleys we boys searched for tomahawks and arrowheads left by our Indian predecessors.

Mineral, plant, animal and man — four kingdoms of nature, all closely interrelated, yet each evolving within its own life-cycle of birth, growth and death. Here the conifers and ferns had taken their substance from soil and air, and now after tremendous periods of time were returning it as coal, graphite, gas and oil — to warm our houses, provide our pencil lead, cook our food and fuel the furnaces of industry. Stored carbon — in its elemental form one of the softest of minerals and opaque. Yet with just a little difference of internal structure wrought by the accumulated pressure of the ages, it yields pure carbon still, but now in crystal form, the hardest of minerals, the most beautiful and transparent, a many-faceted diamond.

One in essence, different in body — so the world, after all, from mineral to star is of the same basic stuff. It is simply a question of what is done with 'matter,' how its particles are arranged or combined, to make at one stage a weed, at another a stone or a man, or again a sun. The durability and versatility of the life-force — I have never lost that youthful flash of conviction. There is a brotherhood that embraces the whole of cosmos, not only human beings but everything from electron to nebula. And all the peoples of the globe are kin literally, and neither their color of skin nor the languages they use can make or unmake that fact. *We are one:* chemically, fashioned of star-stuff cosmically diffused; spiritually, sparked with the flame of a divine element that ignites every point in space into an evolving unit.

If there is indeed "a divinity that shapes our ends," how account then for the sickness of the times? In nearly every direction, there is upheaval, discouragement, a tragic lassitude of spirit. Why should this be so, when never before have we had such magnificent opportunities for development? Are we really heading toward disaster? Or is there some aspect we have neglected because of our absorption in the dark side of human affairs?

"Where the night is blackest, there the stars shine brightest." The old Spanish proverb was rarely more apt. Perhaps we have grown a little too tall too soon. Exploration of outer space has suddenly brought down on us a whole new set of problems which we find ourselves ill equipped to handle all at once. We are being forced to assume the responsibility of a higher adulthood, and we have not as yet fully recognized, let alone accepted, the challenge. But we are learning fast and well. The very upheaval so universally felt is the mark of a strong inward stirring, the struggle of the soul of mankind in the process of shedding an outgrown chrysalis.

Of course we have problems, and serious ones, but I have as little use for the hawkings of the perennial gloom-peddlers as I have for the peace-of-mind addicts who sugar-coat every difficulty. Let us have a realism of the spirit that is not afraid to face life as it is. If we would keep pace with the scientists as they send out their probes, we should be probing the reaches of the inner space within the heart of man that is his link with the divine inspiration that brought the cosmos into being.

We may appear to be little more than developed animals, but given some understanding patience and a little time, we shall find our wings and know that no power in the universe is mightier than the divine essence embedded within us. Mentally and spiritually we are indeed giants in embryo, coequal in potential with the great Intelligence that inspirits the galaxies and suns. That is the realism which will prove far more dynamic than the so-called realism of the negative-minded.

So let us have done with overanxiety and doubt. No one ever succeeded by feeling sorry for himself or by constantly downgrading his inherent capacity to achieve. Certainly we cannot pray away evil any more than we can deny that disease and sorrow and death are part of human experience. But health and joy and growth are also part of living. Viewed from the outer roll of events, the lives of many may seem to be a failure; but, seen through the eyes of our highest self, there can be no failure. No matter how many battles we lose, the immortal Warrior within is invincible and will lead us again and again to the field of human endeavor until full victory is ours.

If Divine Intelligence does pervade every particle of Infinity, then every single human being has at his command all the power and creative initiative to work with it and its constructive elements in nature. We may have plenty of coal and crude oil in our make-up; but we also have the potential of a diamond. That is why the Buddhists, particularly in Tibet, spoke of the Lord Buddha as the "diamond-heart," he whose whole being had through the pressure of the ages and the intensity of experience been metamorphosed into the purity and strength of the diamond. From the most opaque in quality, Gautama became through the crucible of trial the most translucent: as perfect a reflection of the Light from within as of the sorrow of man from without. An exemplar of compassion in very truth, because so adamantine in will and purpose, yet so responsive to the heart-cry of the world, that he refused the bliss of Omniscience that he might return to earth to share the radiance of his triumph with all mankind.

Coal or diamond — we too are compound of both.

The Six Glorious Virtues of Buddhism — I

QUESTION — You have often said that the most profound truths are the simplest, and that they form the backbone of all the great religions. I have given a lot of thought to that. Recently I found a little book, *The Voice of the Silence*, which listed "six glorious virtues." The ideas appeal to me, and I'd like to know more about them.

Comment — I take it you are referring to the Pāramitās of Buddhist literature. They are commonly given as six, though sometimes as seven or even ten, but the number is not so important. I feel it would take us too far afield to go at length into them, but we can certainly discuss them.

Every great religion contains precepts or exhortations toward a better life. In Buddhism the Pāramitās are a set of "Virtues" describing qualities of thought and action which, if made a part of one's life, will reveal the mysteries of the universe and of man. It has also been said that their practice by the sincere aspirant will lead ultimately to complete enlightenment. In other words, the Pāramitās, truly lived, point the way to direct perception of truth. The same could be said of any group of qualities or Virtues. If we *lived* the one commandment of Jesus we would get the same result — for perfect love brings perfect understanding.

Question — This is all new to me as I am not familiar with the Buddhist religion. I wonder if you could explain what each of these Virtues means.

Comment — Yes, but let's omit the use of the Sanskrit words, unless in the discussion it seems advisable to analyze a particular term. Translated into English the Pāramitās are as follows:

1. *Charity* — the key of charity and love immortal;
2. *Uprightness* — the key of harmony in word and act;
3. *Forbearance* — patience sweet, that nought can ruffle;
4. *Dispassion* — indifference to pleasure and to pain;
5. *Dauntlessness* — the dauntless energy that fights its way to the supernal truth;
6. *Contemplation* — the open doorway to truth.

I might mention that service to mankind is held of first importance: "To live to benefit mankind is the first step. To practice the six glorious virtues is the second."

Question — Personally, I don't see any special value in

these things. Can we say that the Buddhist has found truth any more successfully than the Christian or the Hebrew? What I mean is: these Virtues sound fine, but I confess they leave me almost as cold as the Ten Commandments; perhaps because I don't see that they get you any closer to *living* than anything else.

Comment — You're right in that as long as any set of rules or code of conduct remains a formula, it is dead — whether it be the Ten Commandments, the six or ten Pāramitās, or the one sublime injunction of the Christ. It is only when a system or code helps us to channel our aspirations that it becomes a bridge to a fuller comprehension of existence.

One of the most difficult things that any of us has to learn is the direct and practical relationship between these ethical precepts and the intellectual understanding of the laws that govern man's inner and outer life and the inner and outer life of the universe. If the history of the soul could be written, perhaps the greatest struggle through unnumbered ages would be seen as that between the desire for knowledge on the one hand, and the yearning of the soul for wisdom on the other. The intellect is essential, but it is not the prime factor in man's development. The experience of every aspirant shows that as soon as he acquires a fair degree of intellectual capacity, the temptation is to become so fascinated with the intricacies of the universe — more exquisite in form than the finest precision instrument — that he loses sight of the soul's true goal: the conscious working with the inner divinity in order to serve the world of man.

In other words, the practice of the Virtues necessary for the attainment of truth too often takes second place to the

intellectual acquisition of facts, and more and more facts —
an avenue that leads to spiritual sterility.

Question — I can appreciate this, as I've always been
skeptical of anything approaching special training. Have
these Virtues anything to do with psychism?

Comment — Not at all. Any system or method of "training" that even remotely fringes on the psychic tends to lead
the soul away from truth. There is too much running after
this sort of thing nowadays. People think they are becoming spiritual by dabbling in these so-called "occult arts," but
all they are doing is actually hindering their own development. True occultism is altruism per se, and has nothing to
do with psychism. The Pāramitās stress the development of
the *spiritual* qualities of our nature as contrasted with the
psychical and purely mental, and thus are linked directly to,
because an integral part of, that urge in every human being
who has his eyes looking to the divinity within.

Spiritual understanding and wisdom come only as the
natural result of the day to day living of the spirit behind
these "virtues" or "commandments" or "codes of ethics,"
whether they are Hindu, Christian or Buddhist, and whether
they are enumerated as one, three, four, seven or ten. For it
is the essence of these formulas or guides that is the enduring
force, not their outer vehicle; and it is the qualities behind
them that we want to discuss, not their particular form.

Question — That's a pretty big order. I myself couldn't
begin to live one of them, much less all six. How do you
start? Should we try to master each one, and then go on to
the next? I'm afraid I'd get stuck on the first and never get
to the others.

Comment — You cannot isolate any one of these Virtues and practice it fully without bringing into play, at least in degree, all of the other qualities. Nature doesn't work that way — everything contributes to everything else, and everything contributes to the whole. Again, let us not pin our attention too closely on their form, because they will then become for us a dead thing so far as any spiritual values are concerned.

You will remember that the first requirement was "to live to benefit mankind." That was called the "first step," not the second, fourth or fifth, but the first step; while the practice of the Virtues was called "the second step." That is a most significant distinction. As we think about it, we shall realize that the very aspiration to live so that the entire current of one's life is truly a service will automatically prepare oneself to begin the practice of at least some of the Virtues, if not all of them. And as we orient our thinking and our lives we shall see that these Virtues can represent a natural opportunity to transmute the base metal of our natures.

Let us take the first one: *Charity* and love immortal. This word charity has been grossly misapplied, for in its original sense it did not mean pity in the negative, limiting, and even unkind manner we too often employ it. Rather it denoted a spontaneous welling up of understanding and regard for the need of a brother. It comes close to us in every relationship of life, from the simplest to the most complex, because contact with others forces us to choose: either to take a step toward the selfish path, or toward the selfless, compassionate path. True charity does not make known its intent — when you do alms, do them "in secret." The practice of Charity is true consideration and thought for others; it pulls us away from an overconcern with ourselves, and thus sets a keynote for all the other virtues.

Question — Isn't it simply the Golden Rule in action? And wasn't it Paul who said something to the effect that even if we speak with the tongue of angels but have not charity, then we are as "sounding brass or a tinkling cymbal"?

Comment — Exactly so; and every world scripture, if we know how to read it, stresses this same altruistic approach.

So much for the first Virtue or Pāramitā. The second one, *Uprightness* or "harmony in word and act," follows along naturally, and tells us in what manner we must conduct ourselves while putting into practice our ethics.

Question — That one bothers me more than the first one. "Harmony in word and act" — does that mean you have always to give in to others, in discussion or argument, just because you want peace? Peace at any price has become quite a talking point these days.

Comment — That is not the view I take. "Peace at any price" to my mind is one of the most ineffectual if not disastrous means of gaining true and lasting peace. But let us not get into social or political questions here, not because we are afraid of them, but because it is so easy to get into intellectual arguments without resolving a thing.

To get back to this second Pāramitā: Uprightness implies harmony, but not necessarily agreement. There is quite a difference when we think about it. You cannot produce harmony if everyone plays the same note. The composer uses several tones, dissonances and even discords, and then resolves them into a harmonious arrangement. That is what symphony means, the bringing together of sounds, the harmonizing of several different tones. So Uprightness implies the living in accord with our higher resolves, and hence reflecting in our daily activities a harmony in word and act. In simple words, living in such a way that we do not offend the balance and arrangement of natural law.

The only reason we suffer, whether mentally, physically or emotionally, is that somewhere along the line we have disturbed the cosmic equilibrium, and caused inharmony in one or more of its many forms — and too often discord in our relations with others. Nature then reacts, automatically and impersonally, and attempts to readjust the equilibrium we had disturbed. Therefore we suffer. But as we become more able to work in sympathetic relationship with her laws, we find that we do not constantly stir up whirlpools of strife and disorder, but actually are able quietly to re-establish harmony.

Now let us go to the third Virtue: *Forbearance*. It doesn't take much to realize that a little more patience in the world would help things along. As said, we cannot look at these Pāramitās as a progressive series of steps, like the rungs of a ladder. In a way, they do follow each other naturally, but you couldn't possibly practice one to any degree without practicing in some measure the others.

As for needing patience: again, that is double-edged in its application. We have to learn discrimination here as well as in all other lines of endeavor. "Patience is a virtue" has been drummed into our ears since childhood. It is most assuredly a virtue, and a necessary one; but we all know there are times when it is the part of wisdom as well as strength to stop allowing others to impose upon us.

It looks as though we're not going to be able to finish the Pāramitās, so let me run quickly through the others to give us a picture as to how they all fit together:

4. *Dispassion* — indifference to pleasure and pain;

5. *Dauntlessness* — that dauntless energy to fight for truth;

6. *Contemplation* — becoming thoroughly absorbed in the atmosphere of our effort;

all of which lead to *Direct Perception* or *Self Knowledge*.

That in brief sums up the Pāramitās. I must repeat that all of this means absolutely nothing if we don't apply the essential quality of these Virtues. Unless the vital spiritual force flows into and through every thought and action and feeling of our lives, they are indeed as tinkling cymbals and as sounding brass.

We can know all the Sanskrit terms, be able to define the root-meanings, understand intellectually the *modus operandi* of spiritual enlightenment, or think we do, but when Life suddenly takes us at our word and says "prove the worth of these Virtues in your daily experiences" — we shall fail utterly if we have not made their inner quality a part of our very soul.

Question — It seems easy to resolve all of this nicely on a conversational level, but really to live and act without looking for results, without trying to see the fruits of our acts, is something else entirely. By indefatigably following this course, we would find ourselves on a hairline of action and motive. In short, to *live* it on the plane of day to day experiences is a horse of another color — at least to me it is.

Comment — That is where the great beauty of it all is. If it were easy, we wouldn't bother. But it is not easy, and yet it is beautifully simple too. That is where the paradox lies. It is pretty rugged when you stop to think that the truths we are all seeking will not become ours until we start actually putting some of these basic virtues into practice, not only on Sundays or on Wednesdays, but every hour of every day. We all have wondered about this, just why it was so; but the more we make them a part of our brooding consciousness, the more assured do we become that it couldn't work any other way. For the secrets of nature are not given at random, but only after the necessary preparation and training. As one great teacher put it: "It is he who has the love of humanity at heart, who is capable of grasping thoroughly the idea of a regenerating practical Brotherhood who is entitled to the possession of [nature's] secrets. He alone, such a man — will never misuse his powers, as there will be no fear that he will turn them to selfish ends."

The secrets of nature are not secret as such, but a way of life that will not be revealed until we fulfill the true mission of the soul — that of service here in the world.

The Six Glorious Virtues — II

QUESTION — Could we start with the fourth Pāramitā which you called "indifference to pleasure and pain"? I have been thinking about it, but I can't see the logic in becoming indifferent. Of course, if we all want to be hermits, that's one thing; but I've always felt we should be pretty well aware of everything if we want to understand the other fellow's problems. Why should we try to escape from either pleasure or pain?

Comment — Certainly we do not want to escape from our responsibilities by becoming hermits and trying to find quick salvation for ourselves. That is far from the true aspirant's goal. In fact, we shouldn't try to run away from anything, much less from the problems that pleasure and pain bring. That would be escapism pure and simple – and of a most selfish kind. However, even if for a time we succeeded, we couldn't run away for very long, for the "pairs of opposites," heat and cold, night and day, pleasure and pain, or north and south, are intrinsic in nature.

Let me read the full definition of this fourth Virtue: *Dispassion* – "indifference to pleasure and pain, illusion conquered, truth alone perceived." When we see things as they really are, not as they appear to be, then the truth of a situation will be perceived.

Question – Would you define the word *dispassion?* It seems important to get down to basic meanings.

Comment – Let us see what the dictionary says: "*dispassion* – freedom from passion; *dispassionate:* free from passion; not carried away; calm, impartial; synonyms: cool, collected, serene, unruffled." An excellent definition to my mind. We can say then that dispassion is the quality of viewing any situation or condition of life with an impartial eye, hence with clarity of vision, because the clouds of passion or illusion, whether of overelation or depression, have been dispersed.

Thus, this fourth Virtue does not advocate *escape* from the pairs of opposites; but rather the practice of calm indifference to the *effects* on ourselves of either pleasure or pain so that we can meet with equanimity whatever extremities life has in store.

Question – Wouldn't it be rather a dull existence if we never experienced the extremes? What about the highly sensitive person? One day he is way up in the clouds of rapture, and the next sunk in despair. Still he is *living*, not just having a nondescript life, without either joy or sorrow.

Comment — I can assure you there's nothing nondescript about trying to put this particular Virtue into practice. As one wit expressed it: it may be a child's school, but it takes a man to go through it. Try for one week to meet every event, from morning to night, with equanimity, and see if it doesn't take a lot of moral strength to sustain the effort. To be sure, there are people in every walk of life who are so insensitive they don't feel anything, and what is more, don't give a hoot about the suffering of others. Fortunately they are in the minority. Of course it is not for us to judge the inner sensitivity of another, however crude or apparently insensitive his personality may be.

There are, on the other hand, those individuals, and geniuses too, who feel everything with intense keenness. While I am not holding a brief for the irregular life of many a genius, still the world would be the loser if a few had not had those moments of pure vision, and attempted in their way to bring back a memory of "truth alone perceived." But the genius is in a category all his own, and it is highly questionable whether that is the right and natural pathway for the majority of mankind. Most of us are just ordinary folk — neither reprobate nor genius — who in our better moments try to find that "golden mean" or, as the Buddha phrased it, that "middle" course where spiritual growth can go hand in hand with, if not lead, our material development. To be dispassionate then is to be free from the dominance of any particular desire. Obviously, such indifference or dispassion must apply first and foremost to ourselves, for it would be contrary to the compassionate law of Being if we felt a callous indifference to the pain of others.

Question — I find this particular Virtue gives me the most trouble, because I think I would be dead if I didn't have any dominating desires.

Comment — But to strive after "indifference to pleasure and pain" does not mean you shouldn't have desire! It simply means that we have to try to live in the *center* of every experience, rather than swinging so far on the pendulum of life that we hit our head (and heart too) first at one end and then rebound violently toward the other. We are enjoined here to try to live and work without succumbing to the *effects* of either pleasure or pain, beauty or ugliness, or any of the pairs of opposites. There is the whole key, as I see it. Certainly we must have desire — it is the powerhouse of evolution. There is an ancient saying from the Vedas: "Desire first arose in IT" — and the world came into being; the divine seed of a world-to-be had first to feel the pulsing flame of desire to manifest before it could assume material form. So with every last one of us: we have to experience the desire to grow, to evolve, otherwise we are supine. The gods know only too well that supine individuals will never make their mark in spiritual (or even in material) things.

Question — Doesn't the Bible say something about the Lord spewing the lukewarm out of his mouth?

Comment — In *Revelation*, I think. No, there's nothing flabby or lukewarm about trying to practice this Pāramitā!

Question — I recently received a letter from a friend who does private duty nursing. She wrote how "sad life was" — she had given her very best, and yet her patient, whom she had come dearly to love, had died. And so it goes on, she wrote: "patient after patient: some get well; others drag through life in misery; and still others don't 'make the grade,' but die." It seems easy to grasp the principles when we discuss them here, but when you have to make them work day in and day out under rather trying circumstances a different set of values comes into play.

Comment — This points up the fine distinction between mere theory and practice. It would be the height of hypocrisy if we didn't feel the sorrow of others as well as their happiness. We must become ever more sensitive to their joy and pain in direct proportion as we become insensitive to our own. That is the first requirement.

But let's go back to the nurse, or better still, the physician or surgeon. He treats patient after patient: through self-discipline and impersonal dedication to his profession he actually lives this fourth Virtue, to a greater or less degree: if he did not have a measure of *indifference*, of "divine carelessness," and trust that if he does his level best he can do no more — he would crack up. He couldn't stand the terrific strain. With all due respect to his talents, his knowledge, and his skill, there is "the hand of God" or karma if you like — and the patient either makes it or not.

Every physician takes the oath, pledges himself to preserve life and to bring health where ill-health is, so far as his ability and knowledge permit. There is small doubt in my mind that the surgeon who operates must suffer greatly when some unforeseen element steps in — and instead of a successful outcome the patient dies. What does he do? He may be painfully hurt — but *walk on* he must. There are other lives to save; other men and women whose happiness and future depend upon his skill, his dedication, his impersonal service. So, with a divine "indifference" to the *effects* of either joy or sorrow, he gives of himself fully to the next patient — without too great an attachment to the success or failure of his efforts.

Question — You are speaking of the ideal physician, because all are not as impersonal, or as dedicated as the one you describe.

Comment — Obviously, every profession, every religious organization, every line of human endeavor will have grand exponents, as well as its selfish, callous and even cruel representatives. But that doesn't undercut the principle. We can act positively, impersonally, with sensitivity to the inner values, as far as we may feel them, in whatever field of action we find ourselves. Doing this, we discover the benefits of putting these Pāramitās into practice.

Question — It all seems very wonderful, but to be able to meet the complex problems of everyday existence with equanimity, isn't that an almost impossible task?

Comment — It isn't easy, by any means. But it is not intended that we shall overnight become "equal-minded as the sage." The Pāramitās are given as an ideal, something to hold within the heart toward which to aspire. I might add that there are certain basic keys which, if understood, do give one not only perspective but a larger self-confidence.

We have talked here again and again about the divinity that resides in the heart of every creature on earth. We tend to forget that that means man too. Once we start to work with that idea, we very soon realize there must be an endless horizon of experience ahead of us, just as there is an endless background of experience behind us. The ancient belief that man is a pilgrim of eternity, with the opportunity to grow and to learn during a series of lifetimes, opens wide the frontier before our consciousness. And the realization comes that the best preparation in the world is given us every hour of the day, for nothing comes to us but that which we ourselves have earned. When we learn to read the daily lesson that life brings us, we shall find opportunities placed before us to appreciate all of the Virtues — not alone the fourth one.

Now the fifth Pāramitā is called *Dauntlessness* — that "dauntless energy that fights its way to the supernal truth, out of the mire of lies terrestrial." This points up the eternal struggle between light and darkness, truth and falsehood. Truth *is*, but to find it the soul needs all the fortitude it can muster to disentangle itself from the jungle of false concepts it has built through the ages. If it can withstand the subtle disguise of deception and the corroding influence of doubt on every plane of experience, then it will *know* truth — not in fullness but in ever greater clarity.

The sixth Virtue is called *Contemplation* — the gateway to truth — the becoming absorbed in its atmosphere, with one's consciousness pondering the eternal values rather than trivial details. There is a world of difference between genuine contemplation and the so-called "practices of meditation," many of which are an actual danger to the soul. In fact, when I am asked "how shall I meditate?" my invariable reply is: "If I were you, I would stop all set practices of meditation." Anything unnaturally forced is a deterrent, rather than an aid, to spiritual growth. I like to think of contemplation as an inward, almost unconscious brooding with the soul-part of us reaching toward the Father within, so that our consciousness will be guided by true values rather than by false.

There in brief are the "six glorious virtues" or "Pāramitās of perfection"— not that their practice leads to perfection, for there is no such thing. But they can, if the *spirit* of them becomes a part of our lives, help us to a broader and more universal understanding.

Question — You said sometimes they are given as ten. I can't see the need for so many or why any further breakdown is necessary. I suppose anyone could draw up a list of six, ten or even thirty virtues. But if the basic idea is absorbed, haven't we enough to work on? Doesn't the desire for information have a habit of breeding desire for more and more facts, so that it piles up on itself? You sometimes wonder if you're ever going to be satisfied until you meet the ultimate answer face to face. It's a kind of selfishness in its own way, isn't it?

Comment — The desire for more and more information unrelated to ethics does indeed breed a sort of selfishness. Yet it is a natural stage of growth, once we have acquired a degree of intellectual capacity, to want more and more facts laid before us in a precise and orderly manner. As we have said, those facts won't do us a bit of good unless we grasp their underlying spiritual values and allow them to keep a close check on our craving for intellectual power.

178

Let me close with the following, taken from a Buddhist scripture, in answer to the question as to how true charity should be practiced:

> When they [students or disciples] are doing acts of charity they should not cherish any desire for recompense or gratitude or merit or advantage, nor any worldly reward. They should seek to concentrate the mind on universal benefits and blessings that are for all alike, and by so doing will realize within themselves the highest perfect wisdom.

In those few words, we have the answer, I do believe, to the real value of whatever code of ethics we might choose to follow.

The Royal Road of Service

QUESTION — Since we discussed the Pāramitās, I have been delving further into Buddhist thought. Most of it I like very much, but I don't understand all this talk about Nirvāna. It seems that the whole purport of Buddhist teaching is to get away from what they call the "Wheel of Life," the succession of lives on earth, in order to attain the bliss of Nirvāna. When I first heard of reincarnation, I thought it was a wonderful idea, and I still do, because it answers so many of my problems. So why should we want to escape the wheel of rebirth? Why this emphasis on bliss?

Comment — I quite agree with you that too much emphasis is placed on the idea of attaining Nirvāna, or whatever term you want to use. Let us not forget when we look into some of these Eastern scriptures that there is as much crystallized thinking in the Orient as there is in the Occident. What the Buddha taught is one thing, but what his followers through the centuries have formalized as his teachings is often quite something else. In many respects the teachings of Buddhism are highly spiritual; nevertheless a number of gross misinterpretations have become commonly accepted as truth, both in the Hīnayāna and Mahāyāna Schools.

Question — Don't they say that if you live a good life on earth, you will reincarnate in a higher animal, and perhaps a human; but if you have lived an evil life, then you will return as a jackal or a snake or leopard?

Comment — That's a perfect example of what I am trying to bring out. Gautama Buddha — one of the loftiest spiritual lights the world has ever seen — did not teach that the human soul would reincarnate in an animal form; for that would be directly contrary to the facts of nature. But because the ancients often used figures of speech or allegorical language to depict certain truths, later generations took the form of the teachings literally, and so misinterpretations became firmly fixed in the minds of the populace.

What the Buddha did teach was that a man must guard with care his every thought and feeling, because these would leave their mark not only upon his character, but upon every life-atom of his constitution. And as "like attracts like," those life-atoms of gross quality after death might easily be attracted, temporarily at least, to the bodies of animals. So

182

too, when the *Upanishads,* and Plato also on occasion, said that a man may be reborn as an animal, they really meant that if the soul is stamped with certain animal propensities these, if not handled, would tend to hold it down in succeeding lives.

One thing is sure: the human soul is intrinsically so much further evolved than the animal, both in quality and experience, that it could not incarnate in a lower form. The ancient idea, once universally understood, is that as human beings we return to earth periodically after a term of rehabilitation and spiritual refreshment in order to continue our quest for self-conscious union with our divine source.

Question — Why the hurry to get rid of the Wheel of Existence? What is the point of trying to attain Nirvāna now?

Comment — There is not only no point in such endeavor, but it is absolutely a mistaken concept. This overemphasis on attaining Nirvāna has been for centuries one of the greatest drawbacks in Oriental thinking. And now in the West, for those who are coming in contact with Buddhist and Vedantist thought, it is likewise becoming a stumbling block in the path of progress. We hear much these days about "Self-Realization," the Western term for the Vedantist concept of Moksha or "release" from the bondage of earthly care. The very name Self-Realization gives the clue: a path of endeavor motivated by desire for personal salvation. Whether we call it Nirvāna, Bliss or Moksha, the inordinate desire to attain bliss points to a self-centered spirituality as contrasted with that sublime path taught by the Buddha and the Christ — to live wholly in the service of all.

Question — Are there then two paths in spiritual things? I had always thought just the material way of life was contrasted with the spiritual. But now you seem to have divided this spiritual path into two.

Comment — There are indeed two paths in spiritual endeavor. The one is called the "path for oneself," and the other, the "deathless path" or the "path of compassion." The "path for oneself" is that followed by all who seek salvation for themselves — whose most ardent devotees usually yearn to enter some type of life whereby they may leave the turmoil and distraction of earthly existence and attain Nirvāna quickly. The other is the ancient path of compassion, steep and thorny, which is trod by those who would follow in the footsteps of the Christ and the Buddha: the path of altruistic endeavor which seeks wisdom solely that truth and light might be shared with all.

The path of matter tends downward; though we are involved in its atmosphere, there are very few indeed who follow the pull downward to the exclusion of all else. The path of spirit is up and forward always, toward the divinity within. The choice between matter and spirit therefore is clear, regardless of how often we fail to realize our aspirations for the permanent values. However, in spiritual things there will likewise come a forking of the way: either to follow the path for ourselves, or for others.

This concept is well known in the Orient, particularly in those countries where Buddhism has been firmly established for centuries; and that is the reason the populace, by tradition, hold the Bodhisattvas in far greater reverence than they do the Buddhas. To them, the Bodhisattva is one who has reached the point where he could step across the chasm of darkness into Nirvāna, Omniscience, Peace or Wisdom, however you care to describe it, but he refuses so that he might stay behind until the last of his brothers can cross over with him. A Buddha, however, is one who, having reached the portal, sees the light ahead and enters Nirvāna, achieving his well-earned bliss.

Question — When my husband and I were in Japan recently, we took a little time out to visit some of the temples. We saw Bodhisattvas carved in all sizes, some of them very artistic. Would you care to say anything about this?

Comment — Not only in Japan, but in China and those parts of India where Buddhism has taken root, you will find numerous carvings of Bodhisattvas. The ideal of compassion is perpetuated in a few of these statues by the right hand of Bodhisattva reaching toward the wisdom and light and beauty of Nirvāna; while the left hand leans downward toward mankind, in a compassionate gesture of benevolence.

Question — I would like to go back to this word bliss. I confess it is a little disturbing to me. When we think of bliss, I guess we all have a different concept. For a child, it would probably be having all the ice cream he could eat forever and ever; for someone else it might be reaching, after much struggle, the top of a mountain. Perhaps I'm too much of this earth, but it has always seemed cowardly to want to escape to some quiet forest and become a hermit. What is so grand in the attainment of bliss after all, even if you decide later on to renounce it for the world?

Comment — There's nothing grand per se in the achievement of Nirvānic bliss. The terms in the original Sanskrit point to the basic distinction: the one is the *Pratyeka* path, or the path of spiritual aspiration "for oneself"—a purely selfish type of spirituality; the other is the *Amrita* path, or the path that proves "deathless" because it is the path of sacrifice, of compassion, of service.

Let me try to put the matter very simply. Suppose you had an intuition which led you to make some scientific discovery, and which you believed could greatly affect the world for good. You could do one of two things: you could keep it all to yourself so that when you completed it you could put it on the market and make a lot of money. Or you could turn it over to the top scientists that it might be worked on and perfected perhaps even by others, and then made available for the use of mankind. Now you would have every right to keep that invention or discovery to yourself, to patent it and make as much profit on it as you could. You could argue that in the end the world would benefit because you had made the product available. In so doing you would experience a certain personal 'bliss' or satisfaction in having achieved your aims. On the other hand, if you gave freely of your discovery that it might be put into the caldron of scientific testing, would you not be doing the world a far greater service? What then would you experience in the way of inner returns?

Question — If you turn your back on bliss, you actually double your bliss, is that it?

Comment — Only if the motive is as selfless as the deed. That is where the joker in the pack always hides. The by-products of joy in selflessly having contributed the fruits of your intuition for the good of all will far transcend any personal satisfaction you might otherwise have; and in a measure you would touch the fringes of bliss, to use the somewhat hackneyed term. But the moment any one of us does a "deed of mercy" in order to have the proud feeling of being a benefactor, that very moment does the so-called beneficent act turn to ashes.

Question — I'd like to ask a question here. Some time ago when we discussed the practice of the Pāramitās, you said that it is all a matter of relativity; that as we gained a higher set of values we would not be content with our former ones. Would the state of bliss or contentment be relative also? What I mean is, there might be a physical or even a mental bliss. But isn't spiritual bliss something quite apart? Do we as human beings ever attain the state that is comparable to the bliss of Nirvāna?

Comment — There are as many Nirvānas as there are individuals to experience it; just as there are as many states of consciousness right on this earth as there are people living. Those who strive for Nirvāna, for wisdom and light and peace, for themselves alone — remember the term Pratyeka means just that, "for oneself"— think they will attain perfect bliss. But the Buddhas of Compassion and true Bodhisattvas know that they could not possibly attain the full condition of omniscience. Everything is relative. Spiritual omniscience or Nirvānic bliss is an experience so far beyond our power to conceive that it is impossible to describe. Just because we cannot comprehend what this state of omniscient wisdom is, let us never forget that the power to achieve oneness with the Divine lies in the heart of every one.

There are many grades above our present state of humanhood, and there are advanced men who have attained to union with the Father, whether momentarily or for a longer period. They experience a touch of Nirvānic bliss; yet, moved by the compassionate urge to serve mankind, they allow their consciousness to return to the field of human endeavor that they might work among and with humanity.

Question — It is a wonderful picture. I must say there are times when all the distractions and turmoil really impinge too heavily, and we have to get away for a while, climb a mountain, rest by the seaside, or travel a bit, anything to recharge the old batteries. But I've found that after a few weeks I long to get back into the thick of things. Once my nerves get relaxed, up comes that urge to get back in harness. I can't say it's because I've wanted to follow a path of compassion; it's simply that somehow the struggle in life seems more interesting than just lolling around. What would I be headed for — the path that is selfish, or the other one?

Comment — Far be it from me to decide who is on the Pratyeka or selfish path, and who is striving to follow the compassionate path. No one can judge another. Remember it is the motive, the real *inner* motive that is often concealed, and not the outer, that colors one's field of action. Day by day we are making innumerable little choices that will in time, one way or the other, tip the scales of that supreme choice.

We are all human, and if we want to get back into the struggle of existence just to outsmart the other fellow, to get ahead as fast as we can in order to obtain power and influence, then we are heading downward; if we don't check ourselves, but continue in this direction life after life, we will be following the path of matter which leads ultimately to spiritual death. But if after our vacations we return to our jobs because of an inherent desire to do our part in the grand over-all scheme of existence, participating in the joys and sorrows of life as part of our share in lifting the world's burden, then our motive is of selfless origin. Gradually it will become more and more refined, and the ideal of the path of compassion will take firm root in our hearts.

Question — But how do we become spiritual?

Comment — We shouldn't try to become spiritual or holy or advanced, for that very overemphasis of interest in one's own development is the greatest bar to progress. Spiritual attainment is never the result of trying to become spiritual, strange as that may sound. Yet we are enjoined again and again to "raise the lower by the higher self," to transmute the base metal of selfish desire into the gold of selfless endeavor. All of which means that we should ever and always aspire toward the ideal of altruism, of selflessness, and all the other Virtues we have discussed, but not concentrate on our own evolution. Even if we knew the doctrines of Buddhism, Christianity or Platonic thought from A to Z, this in itself would not make us spiritual.

Question — Well, these Pratyekas that you speak of — aren't they spiritual beings? If not, how else could they become Buddhas? I don't understand this combination of selfishness and spirituality. Can there really be selfishness in spiritual achievement, because wouldn't you have to serve as you grew?

Comment — Let us not get the erroneous impression that a Pratyeka, one who works for spiritual things for himself,

is evil. He isn't. He is a highly developed spiritual individual; nor is it correct to say that he would never do anything for his fellowmen. They all do — there is no question
of that, for the simple reason they can't help themselves.
Again we return to motive. I can go out tomorrow and be
a so-called "angel of mercy" and perform all manner of good
works; or if I have plenty of money I can give to charity,
to this or that benevolent cause. But what effect will such
"acts of mercy" have on my character, on my karma, or on
my real Self?

It is not *what* we do that will decide; but *how* we think
and act. In the final judgment one thing only will count:
MOTIVE. If I get a certain satisfaction out of being a benefactor, I will undoubtedly do a lot of good, make many
people's lives better, relieve much distress. Still, if I am doing
these "good works" that I may be the doer of good deeds,
that I may reach my goal of spirituality more quickly — is
there not more than a touch of selfishness in my motive? On
the other hand, if in the smallest acts of daily life I try never
to intrude my personal will into the equation of human relationships, but strive always that the channel of service be
open solely for the benefit of others, then surely the motive
will be selfless. And the results — infinitely more enduring
because they will be felt, not in the personal natures of those
helped, but in the higher portions of their souls where the
benefits will continue through life after life.

Thus you have the two lines of spiritual endeavor: the
one, for the purpose of getting bliss for oneself — the seemingly quicker pathway because the sorrows and trials of
others do not delay one; and the other, for the purpose of
making lighter the sorrow of man.

190

The Pratyeka path in the end becomes the slower path, for once the aspirant reaches the point where he is sufficiently enlightened to have stepped into Nirvāna, he says good-bye to further spiritual growth, remaining static until the next great cycle — which may be a very long period. Ultimately each one of us will have to make the supreme choice, whether to step across the threshold or to glimpse the glory of utter wisdom and peace, yet return to the vale of tears to help mankind. That is the choice of the Great Ones of the race. Theirs is a thankless task. They seek no reward, no credit, nothing but the opportunity to share of their own hard-won wisdom.

That is why the pure tradition is born of and passed on by the line of Compassionate Ones, who take no thought for their own advancement because they have at heart the interest of their fellowmen.

To offer all action on the altar of one's own progress is Pratyeka — selfish in the final testing; to offer all thought, action and feeling on the altar of humanity's progress — that is Compassion in its highest expression.

Our Divine Potential

In the Mystery-schools, those ancient centers of training that the philosophers attended in order to learn things not ordinarily given out, the complete constitution of both man and the universe was studied. That is why in the days of the ministry of the Master Jesus he said to his disciples: to the multitudes I speak in parables, but to you I reveal the Mysteries.

Sometimes man was divided into four elements, at other times into five, but more generally either the three basic principles were stressed, as did St. Paul, or they were expanded into seven. The particular method used is secondary to the fact that all Scriptures tell the selfsame story of God or Divinity periodically manifesting a part of Itself, a portion of Its qualities, for the benefit of all creation. That is why we are here: to give our individual god-spark an opportunity to have further experience through what we may call the hierarchies of life. That god-spark is the very highest pinnacle of our being, but at this stage in our evolution has many encasements of varying degrees of materiality.

Since it is a help to compare our accustomed way of viewing man and his nature with the methods of other sacred scriptures, let us expand the usual threefold concept into the sevenfold. An example of this is found in the *Katha-Upanishad*, one of the Thirteen Principal Upanishads (there are numerous minor ones) which have been translated from the Sanskrit into English by Western scholars. They comprise discourses on the ancient traditions that have been handed down for the guidance of mankind — the word *upanishad* meaning "to sit down near," that is, to give one's close attention to the narrator.

Here the symbol of a chariot is used to explain the nature of man. The master of the chariot is the divine Self; the driver or charioteer is the spiritual will, the intuition; and the reins represent the human will, the mind. The horses are the desires and senses; the roads over which the horses draw the chariot are the objects of our sense-desires, while the chariot itself stands for the body, the vehicle of our personality on earth. This to me is a striking analogy because of the entirely fresh light it throws on our struggles.

> Know the Self (*ātma*) as the master sitting
>   within the chariot which is the body (*śarīra*),
> Know again the understanding (*buddhi*) as the charioteer
>   and the mind (*manas*) as the reins.

He who is ever of unrestrained mind,
    devoid of true understanding,
His sense-desires then become uncontrollable
    like the wild horses of a charioteer.

But he who is ever of controlled mind,
    and has true understanding,
His sense-desires then are controllable
    like the good horses of a charioteer.

The desires are superior to the senses,
    the mind is superior to the desires,
The intuition (understanding) is superior to the mind,
    the great Self is superior to the intuition.

                — Chapter III, verses 3, 5, 6, 10

Simply put, the enlightened man, the charioteer, restrains the horses or sense-desires by intelligent manipulation of the reins, the mind, bringing the senses under the guidance of the intuition or spiritual self, and keeping the chariot on the course indicated by the master of the chariot, the divine Self. We see at once that man is not only guided by his mind but may receive, if he will, the guidance and protection of his Father within. To the degree that our human will obeys the impulses of the charioteer, it will be the servant of the spiritual forces of our nature; just as the charioteer or intuitional aspect is the direct servant of the divine will, the master of the chariot.

Now what does all this mean? Viewing man in relation to the larger picture, the prime factor is that this spark of godhood, the master of the chariot, is at the root of all evolutionary effort. Within man is the power to choose — and we can be certain that the way ahead, whether smooth or rough, will be the very roadbed of experience that we need in order to bring into expression our divine potential.

Man — Part Atom, Part Galaxy

QUESTION — Last term several of us students met together once a week, and we had some lively sessions, our views ranging from the most materialistic and even atheistic to the metaphysical. But always we ended up against a stone wall. Regardless of our scientific knowledge, or what our religious backgrounds were — there were a few non-Christians among us — the one question remained unanswered: who is man?

Comment — Who is man? If we knew who we are, from the divine core of our being to the outermost vehicle, the physical body, we would have solved the mystery of *Life* —

197

in all its phases. Why do you suppose the Oracle at Delphi gave answer in those now immortal words — KNOW THY-SELF! Why were they carved over the portal of the temple of Apollo except as a daily reminder that if one would master the secrets of nature, he must first master himself.

If we were to say that man is part atom, part galaxy, we might come as close to the truth as St. Paul did when he told the Corinthians that in man there is a "natural body" (*psyche*) and a "spiritual body" (*pneuma*), and that the first Adam "was made a living soul; the last Adam was made a quickening spirit." We rather glibly speak of ourselves as being composed of body, soul and spirit, but we do not really know what this means. Actually we are far more than this; mind, intuition, desire, all sorts of qualities, make up man.

Question — That was just the difficulty. We tried to compare the New Testament with Buddhist philosophy, but we got hopelessly confused. We also delved into Hindu thought, and tried to link what they call the *ātma* or Self with the 'Spirit' of St. Paul, which seemed to work out. But when we got to the ordinary part of us, it summed itself up like this: how can we handle this bundle of forces playing through us? Just who are we and what is our link with the bigger scheme of things? That's what we want to know.

Comment — We must not expect at once to know all the particulars regarding the evolution of man, or of the universe in which we are a necessary part, however insignificant we may feel when compared to the Milky Way. We can perhaps catch a glimpse here and there of the broad panoramic sweep of the process of creation, and by so much sense our kinship with and participation in the eternal Mystery. The birth of man, as much as the birth of a galaxy of stars or an atomic universe, is an act of wonder — and never a prosaic thing.

How then can we handle this bundle of opposing forces in ourselves? Do you remember Paul's letter to the Romans, in which he described the "warring of the members" in man? "For the good that I would I do not: but the evil which I would not, that I do." How universal an experience: the good we feel deep in our hearts we want to do, we often don't do; and those very qualities of character that we know are now beneath us, we still want to indulge in. Why is this?

Man is truly part atom, part galaxy; but there is more to the story of creation than the blending of the atomic and the galactic. From the mysterious interaction of Spirit and Matter there comes forth a 'soul-vehicle' in which every living being finds its natural field of action. Thus in reality all things — from the atomic worlds and sub-worlds, through the mineral, vegetable, animal and human kingdoms, right on out to the galaxies in space — have at least a threefold expression: 'body,' their material form, whether electron or star; 'soul,' their vehicle of consciousness or self-expression, however rudimentary or unaware from the human standpoint this may appear; and 'spirit,' their essential root in Deity.

Question — Do you mean that every one of us really is a portion of God? It is refreshing to feel the vigor of a philosophy that presupposes God as within us. We have for so long been taught of our ape-ancestry; or worse, that we were miserable sinners, worms in the dust from which Adam was formed.

Comment — God or Deity, or a portion of the Divine Intelligence, *is* our root-essence, and were it not for that we would not be here, suffering and enjoying incarnation on this planet in our solar system, and traveling along within the larger destinies of the galaxies which make up the Meta-galaxy in which we, and the tiniest sub-electron, do live and move and have our very life.

But we must not get so far up into the superstellar reaches of thought that we lose our footing on earth! Our present responsibility is to meet here and now the challenge of this rapidly moving age of scientific expansion, and to control and develop the energies of our soul and spirit, our mind and aspirations, so that they will in time radiate clearly the light of the divine sun within us.

Moreover, let us drop from our consciousness forever this "worm in the dust" concept. That is absolutely false, and has no place in the vocabulary of Man, the Thinker. Nor has the ape-ancestry theory ever been proved! There is as much against it, evolutionally speaking, as for it; and far more to disprove it when we view man not as his body but as a flaming Intelligence imbodied on earth in order to learn the lessons of material existence. While it is a fact that our physical constitution has developed slowly through the eons to the highly refined mechanism it is today, neither the Divinity within nor the Promethean fire of our minds could have grown out of an ape! Have we ever considered the possibility of the ape (and the monkeys too) being offshoots of man's indiscretions in the early history of the race? That is what certain ancient traditions suggest; it is worth serious consideration, even from the standpoint of the physical development of the early primates. Why is it that of the mammalia man's body is the most primitive and unspecial-ized, while his mind and the inner energies of his soul have developed in extraordinary ways, and there appear no limits to his power to evolve?

Question — I never thought of it that way before. But where does our mind fit in, and all those strange yet real intimations that we are something more than our ordinary emotions and feelings?

Comment — What makes man different from the atom or the rose? What gives him that sense of awareness of himself, that quality of self-consciousness that separates him from the lower kingdoms, and which makes him at once the despair of himself and the glory of creation? Mind — active, dominant, creative. You recall how the serpent told Eve that if she and Adam would but taste of the fruit from the tree of knowledge they would *not* die, but would become as gods, knowing good from evil. The mind of man was here touched into the flame of awareness by the Promethean ember — itself a spark from the central fire of the cosmic Mind — and the knowledge of right and wrong came into being; and, most important, the recognition of moral responsibility to choose wisely and in harmony with nature.

The point of no return had thus been reached as far as man's evolutionary trek was concerned. No longer could he drift contentedly with the slow-moving rivers of progress. Henceforth he must be up and doing, meeting the challenge of directing his own growth, and by trial and error learn that whatever he sowed he would have to reap, in cycle after cycle of experience. Who then is man? Briefly, he is both Knower and deluder of himself: the choice is his.

Question — What do you mean by that? That we are both Knower and deluder?

Comment — Paul's references to soul and spirit and to man's having a "natural body" and a "spiritual body" told only part of the story. The ancient Greeks viewed man as sometimes having four, and at other times seven qualities; but let us take the four basic principles as they conceived them. Besides *pneuma* or spirit, they spoke of *nous*, which they called the Knower or mind-principle, which in turn used *psyche*, the soul, and *soma*, the body, as its means of growth and experience on earth.

Now it is *nous*, the Knower, which is that portion of man's nature that can command knowledge of himself and of the universe when its energies are directed towards spirit; but when ruled by *psyche*, it becomes the deluder. The old saying "Mind is the slayer of the Real" is at times all too true because, when influenced by the lower emotions, the deluder is in charge, and cunning, greed and tyranny in many forms take possession.

Mind thus is bipolar; at once the slayer and the liberator. A broader knowledge of the spectrum of qualities which make up man, and which likewise flow through the cosmos, is required if we are properly to relate ourselves to the earth on which we live, and understand intelligently how to meet all these forces that impinge upon us.

Question — That is a very intriguing phrase: spectrum of qualities. Do you mean that we are composed of *seven* qualities, like the seven colors of the spectrum?

Comment — Why not? We may even speak of ten as the ancient Egyptians did, but let us use the seven as it harmonizes easily with what we are familiar with in nature, such as the seven notes of the scale, the seven colors of the rainbow, the seven days of the week, etc. What were these seven principles of man called? By various names, which can be rendered something like this: the divine; the spiritual-intuitional; the mental — itself bipolar, with its higher part aspiring toward the spiritual, its lower aspect leaning toward the next 'color' in succession, called desire; then the vital life-forces, which in turn enliven the model-body or blueprint on which the physical body, cell by cell, is built.

Who then is man? Man can rightly be called a spectrum of radiating energies, held together by the dominating essence of his divine core, the Father within, which in turn is rooted in the cosmic Divine Intelligence which pervades every living unit in space.

It is significant that our word spirit is the Latin word for breath, coming from *spiro*, to breathe, just as the Greek *pneuma* also means breath or spirit. Now several of the archaic philosophies conceived of the great Outbreathing and Inbreathing of Deity as the Days and Nights or periods of Activity and Rest of worlds. Thus Motion was the essential characteristic of Deity, and when God wished to bring forth a universe, the 'spirit' of the Elohim (literally, *rūahh*, breath) moved over the face of the Deep; the breath of divine life quickened into manifestation this whole universe, and all the sleeping seeds of divine force, whatever their grade, were breathed forth from Darkness into Light.

Question — This throws quite a different light on our Christian teachings. That verse we had to learn from *Genesis:* And the Lord God formed man of the dust and breathed into him the breath of life. How does that relate to St. Paul's statements, and also to the seven qualities of man?

203

Comment — "And the Lord God formed man of the dust of the ground, and breathed into his nostrils the breath of life (*neshāmāh*); and man became a living soul (*nephesh*)." In the first two chapters of *Genesis* are references to three distinct qualities of breaths or outbreathings from Deity or the Lord God: *neshāmāh*, the "breath of life" corresponding generally to the *pneuma* or "spiritual body" of Paul; *rūahh*, the breath or spirit of the Elohim which brings forth the world, and in man is the quickener of self-conscious life, hence often linked with the Greek *nous*, the Knower; and *nephesh*, the "living soul," analogous to the *psyche* or "natural body" or ordinary human soul; all three breaths or qualities holding together and in-spiriting the shell or physical body.

Now relating this to the seven qualities or spectrum of energies which is man, we could say that St. Paul's 'body' comprises the three lowest: the vital forces, animating the astral matrix, or model-body, around which the physical form patterns itself. The 'soul' may be said to embrace the fields of desire, emotion and mind, but not the highest reaches of mind; while the 'spirit,' as a ray from the divine essence, is the spiritual-intuitional principle, itself powerless to function on earth unless united with mind for a workable vehicle of expression.

When we know that the chemical elements on earth are found likewise in the body of the sun, is it so difficult to imagine that if one could take a spectrograph of the energies of a man's soul and spirit, as well as his mind, desires and aspirations, the *identic* lines would show up on the spectrograph of the *inner* energies of the solar god that animates the physical orb? If the old Hermetic axiom is correct —

"As it is below, so it is above"— then surely the same fundamental energies ranging from the divine to the physical in man must likewise enliven and flow through every manifested thing. All the evidence of logic and analogy points to the selfsame spectrum of qualities throughout the entire cosmos: octaves of radiant energy, expanding out into the depths of space, and inwards into the worlds within worlds of the atom.

Question — Science has moved forward so swiftly that we know a tremendous amount about the galaxies at one end of the gamut of life, and also about the intricacies of the atomic world, but we find it hard to achieve perspective with this constant acceleration of knowledge. How do you think St. Paul would have handled our situation with his correspondents?

Comment — No one could say, but I really do not think he would have been over-alarmed. He probably would have urged us to face the basic issue: will we succumb to the "earth, earthy," that self-centered portion of ourselves which leads downward; or will we rise to the demands of the Knower within and live creatively, dedicating our knowledge to noble ends? A healthy reappraisal of man and his place in a growing and living universe has been long overdue.

The mind itself is a dynamo of radiant force, and when held in check by the spiritual and intuitional energies can inspire to enlightened thought and action. But as we know only too well, the lower tendencies of mind allow the desires to pull it hither and yon, so that the horses of our senses get the bit in their teeth and run wild. As the *Upanishad* said, in the chariot sits the master within, the divine essence, and

205

it is up to us to see to it that the charioteer or spiritual-intellectual driver wisely holds the reins of our mind so that the horses of our desires will lead us in the direction of our true goal.

If science and its immensely enlarged fields of study had done nothing more than take off our theological blinkers, it would have earned the gratitude of the Protectors of mankind, that long line of spiritual Titans who come periodically, as did Krishna, Christ and Buddha, to reawaken in man his spiritual vision and stimulate anew his longing for truth. Our new knowledge of the universe is providing increasing evidence that, however much a part of us is clothed with the "dust" of earth, we are in truth a "quickening spirit."

Theosophia — Knowledge of Things Divine

Q UESTION — The other day a friend suggested I look into theosophy. He said he didn't know too much about it, and there were a lot of different opinions as to its merits and even some rather contradictory presentations, but he believed that basically it had some good philosophy behind it. So I was wondering whether we could go into its background.

Comment — All right, but first let us ask ourselves what we mean by theosophy. Do we mean its modern form that finds expression today in the several organizations that call themselves theosophical? Do we mean the theosophy of the Middle Ages or of the Renaissance? Or thinking still farther back, are we referring to the period of Ammonius Saccas who lived in the second and third centuries of our era? Again, do we have in mind the archaic philosophy of the early Mystery-schools? Or, coming closer to our own times, are we speaking of the type of Christian theosophy that found an outlet in the life and writings of Jakob Boehme who in turn inspired the "theosophers" of the seventeenth, eighteenth and nineteenth centuries?

Question — I had no idea there were so many kinds of theosophy or that it reached so far into the past. I thought it was a modern word for a new kind of philosophy.

Comment — No, theosophy is not a newfangled thing, though unfortunately much that has gone under its name, in former times as well as today, concerns the husks rather than the kernel of its philosophy. The whole subject has so many ramifications that, in order to sketch even a bare outline of its development and growth, we should have to research into its origins and then thread our way carefully through the tangled web of differing connotations that the term 'theosophy' has accumulated in the process of time. The word is believed to go back to the first few centuries of our era, and possibly earlier, while its usage, though limited, predates by hundreds of years the establishment of the modern organizations that bear the name and which, with varying fidelity to its original significance, profess to follow a theosophic philosophy.

I would ask just one thing, that we try to hold in abeyance any current notions we may have about what theosophy is and what it is not, so that we can more easily trace its development.

Question — I would like that very much, because I also thought it was a kind of new philosophy or creed. But what does the word mean?

Comment — It's from the Greek. Let's start with the dictionary definition and proceed from there.

THEOSOPHY. Also *theosophism*. From ML., fr. LGr. *theosophia*, knowledge of things divine, fr. *theosophos*, wise in the things of God, fr. *theos*, God + *sophos*, wise. . . .

So much for the actual derivation of the word. Incidentally, I don't believe the word "theosophism" was ever used much, though it does appear occasionally in the writings of certain "theosophers" of some two hundred years ago.

Note the symbols: "From ML., fr. LGr." — these, of course, signify that the word comes through Medieval Latin from Late Greek; that is, the type of Greek spoken from the first or second to the sixth century A.D. Right here, in a moment's time, we make a big leap in thought through the Dark Ages of our history back to those turbulent transition centuries following the beginning of the Christian era. You can see, therefore, what folly to confine our discussion of theosophy merely to modern times. But let us continue with the two definitions which follow the derivation of the word itself:

1. Alleged knowledge of God and of the world as related to God obtained by direct mystical insight or by philosophical speculation or by a combination of both.

2. (*often capitalized*) The doctrines and beliefs of a modern school or sect following, in the main, Buddhistic and Brahmanic theories, especially in teaching a pantheistic evolution and the doctrine of reincarnation.

Question — That sounds rather complicated. How can anyone really have "knowledge of God"?

Question — I want to know if God is capitalized there. I seem to be confused. First we get the translation of the word as "knowledge of things divine," which I like. It gives one a feeling of no limits. But then we're told that theosophy means "alleged knowledge of God." And right away I begin to feel hemmed in by the idea of a Personal Deity about whom theosophy is supposed to tell me. Perhaps I'm just splitting hairs.

Comment — No, I don't think you are. In fact, you have put your finger on something which we might peruse for a moment. Yes, God is capitalized in both phrases — "wise in the things of God," and "alleged knowledge of God." Had the lexicographers translated *theos* as "a spiritual or divine being" or simply as "divinity," which were its connotations in Greek times, instead of adopting the later Christian usage of God, they would have come much closer to the essential significance of *theosophia* as "knowledge of divine things." Nevertheless, the fact that they inserted the word *alleged* shows that they were well aware that no human being could be fully "wise in the things of God," much less comprehend the boundless wisdom of a Divine Intelligence whose experience includes the alpha and omega of life itself on our planet, our solar system and indeed within and beyond our home-universe.

As said, the first definition treats of theosophy as variously used in preceding centuries, and is written with a small *t*. But the second definition, "often capitalized," pertains to the "modern school" of thought bearing the name theosophical. To make a point of this distinction may seem somewhat irrelevant, but it is not. The history of man's development and progress in true spiritual insight has proven time and again that the moment we put our beliefs in 'capitals' we specialize and become static; the moment we specialize, we limit; and when we limit we begin to lose the very essence of that which we are seeking. In physical or administrative matters, we must of necessity define a problem in order to focus our attention on this or that specific area of interest. But when we treat of "divine things" that pertain to the growing inner constitution of man and of the cosmos, we are dealing with non-static developing principles of truth, whether we call them Buddhism or Christianity, Neoplatonism or theosophy. By placing those principles within the framework of finality, we have limited their significance to the particular form that our definitions take.

This is the case whether we are considering the *gnosis* (knowledge) of gnostic theosophy, the theosophic speculations of the Hebrew Kabbalists or of the Fire-Philosophers, the Christian theosophy expounded by Meister Eckhart, Jakob Boehme or Saint-Martin, or again its modern representations. That is why I suggested we hold in abeyance our previous notions in order that we might enlarge our area of thought, and view theosophy, literally, as "knowledge of things divine." If we can consider it in this sense, we will realize that the *essence* of pure religion and philosophy — and of science too when considered as pure "knowledge" which is what the word means — is *theosophia* with a small *t*, that quality of "wisdom" which the greatest Seers of mankind have attained through direct perception of "things as they are."

Question — May I interrupt? If we follow out that last thought, would it mean then that all the Saviors or world teachers, such as Buddha and Jesus, and I suppose men like Plato and Pythagoras, taught a kind of theosophy?

Comment — Let's not make a new dogma out of this and say that every religion and philosophy is theosophy; we could as easily say they are all Buddhism or Christianity or Islam, and so forth. Nevertheless, you have a point here, because no matter what system of thought we consider, if we can discern its eternal and imperishable quality we will arrive at one central point — truth. Their differences lie only in their external wrappings, which most of the time tend to hide rather than to reveal their essential worth.

This brings us to the second definition, which is capitalized and refers to the modern organization founded in 1875 by H. P. Blavatsky, and which attempted to carry on the work originally started by Ammonius Saccas in the third century of our era. Just as he tried to show that truth was one, and that all religions originally sprang from a common wisdom of antiquity, so her thought-provoking work, *The Secret Doctrine*, was written with that in mind. However, during the succeeding years, the term theosophy has suffered considerably by misuse. There exist several organized bodies that attempt with relative success to disseminate its philosophy. But there are also a few dubious cults using the literature to promulgate a type of teaching which is nothing more than a deviation from the original doctrine, with glamorous emphasis on fringe aspects, such as psychism and other unhealthy brands of phenomenalism — all of which are highly dangerous perversions of spiritual values.

Question — Isn't the very type of mixed-up knowledge current today in our philosophical and religious outlook, and particularly in regard to these psychic matters, almost a replica of what was happening in Alexandria when Ammonius lived? Even at an earlier period the Romans had to enact laws against the practice of mediumship, divination and the making of horoscopes; in fact, against anything that tended in the slightest degree toward the use and development of the "occult arts."

Question — I would like to hear more about the earlier uses of the term theosophy.

Comment — To fix the exact date when the term first came into currency is difficult, though I believe the word *"theosophos,"* or "wise in divine concerns," is found occasionally in the writings of Clement of Alexandria and possibly others of that time. Some authorities, however, lean to the view that it was Ammonius Saccas who more specifically grounded his pupils in 'theosophic' principles.

Question — I read somewhere that he taught a kind of eclectic philosophy by combining ideas from different sources.

Question — You mean by skimming off the cream of the various religions and making a sort of spiritual potpourri? I don't like the word "eclectic," because how can you arrive at a sound philosophy by artificially building it up from bits and pieces?

Comment — Let's not go too fast and end up drawing faulty conclusions. I agree with you that we will never find truth by arbitrarily collecting pieces of it and tacking them together. To interpret the word "eclectic" in that sense is, of course, legitimate, but that is far from what Ammonius Saccas did. While his system of instruction is modernly referred to as "eclectic," in reality he followed a threefold method of arriving at truth: analysis, synthesis and interpretation. With Plato as the foundation, he was able to distill the essence of *sophia* or 'wisdom' from the seemingly conflicting elements in the conglomerate of mystical and religious traditions then current in Alexandria. That is why he is considered the inspiring genius behind the extraordinary revival of interest in the Platonic philosophy, which as Neoplatonism was later so strongly to influence not only Christian psychology but even church theology through St. Augustine. But that is another story!

I think it is difficult for us to realize what that teeming metropolis was like in those early centuries. Here was a thriving center of commerce and trade between the Orient, Asia Minor, Africa and Rome, but it was also the seat of the highest culture and learning, the Museum with its Library being famed particularly for its hundreds of thousands of priceless manuscripts (a goodly portion of which was later destroyed by fanatics). Hindus and Buddhists, Greeks, Jews and Egyptians, Romans and Arabs, as well as the growing body of Christian converts mingled, each eager to sell his 'wares,' material or so-called spiritual. And it was here, in protest against the superficiality of life in general, and the hollowness of much that was expounded as truth, that Ammonius founded his school in which he demanded of his disciples the highest reverence for truth. He was called *theodidaktos* or "god-taught," because it was believed that he had experienced the sacred union of the soul with its

214

divine source. Certainly the nobility of his life acted as a constant reminder to his pupils that if they faithfully lived a self-disciplined life they too, in time, might become *theosophos* or "wise in the things of God."

Question — Did Ammonius write any books?

Comment — He wrote nothing down, any more than did Jesus or Buddha or Socrates.

Question — Then how do we know what he taught?

Comment — In the same way that we know, to a fair degree at least, what all the world teachers, including Jesus, taught: by reading between the lines and behind the words of their followers. Ammonius, in accord with the archaic practice of the Mystery-schools (even though in his time they had become very much degraded), exacted a solemn vow from his disciples never to commit to writing what they would learn. After his death, however, two of them circulated some manuscripts, giving their interpretation of his doctrines. Fortunately, for posterity, one very remarkable individual came to study under Ammonius and later wrote several books giving the essence of the teachings imparted.

Question — Wasn't that Plotinus? If I remember the story correctly, he had been searching everywhere among the many philosophical schools in Alexandria for genuine spiritual instruction, but finding nothing but husks had become despondent. Then a friend told him about Ammonius. As Porphyry, the beloved pupil of Plotinus records it, as soon as he heard Ammonius, he exclaimed: "This is the man I have been seeking." So he stayed on with him some ten or eleven years, and it is said that he too attained moments of union with his Father within.

Comment — We have Porphyry to thank for persuading Plotinus that it was his duty, now that these imperfect because incomplete accounts had come out, to preserve in written form a true interpretation of Ammonius' teaching. It would have been a terrible loss otherwise, for Plotinus seems to have outshone even Plato in his exposition of the ancient theme that everything flows from divinity or *theos*, and that all souls and forms and phases of manifestation must in time consciously strive to return to their divine source. Of course there is much more, but it is easy to see why the *theosophia* of Neoplatonism again and again has tried to find expression in succeeding centuries.

Question — I'm trying to link up the definition of theosophy as "alleged knowledge of God" with the fact that Ammonius apparently achieved a "divine insight."

Comment — Let me reread the definition: "Alleged knowledge of God and of the world as related to God by direct mystical insight or by philosophical speculation or by both." If we rephrase this from the vantage point of what we have just discussed, we will see how remarkably apt it is: *theosophia*, or knowledge of divine things concerning the cosmos and man as expressions of divinity, attainable through direct spiritual perception or by study and reflection, or by a combination of the mind illumined by the intuition.

Question — That's wonderful, but who can attain that outside of people like Ammonius or the great teachers?

Comment — Didn't Plato say something about the soul having been impressed at the dawn of time with knowledge of the great 'Idea,' by which he no doubt meant *sophia* or wisdom, and that it was up to us to 'recollect' that knowledge during our lives on earth? And didn't the Master Jesus say that it was the Father within him that was performing the so-called miracles, and that what he did we could do also?

Question — I like that because during the war years I met individuals of entirely different religious backgrounds and, while I didn't have the opportunity to investigate their beliefs, I became convinced that spiritual worth was no respecter of skin, country or religion. That is why I am so interested in Ammonius' hope to show that there was but one truth. I feel there must be, even for us ordinary people, a kind of natural wisdom we can find.

Comment — Isn't it perhaps that "natural wisdom" within all of us that we are trying to recollect?

Question — I've often wondered why there isn't a common pool of knowledge from which we could all draw. I can't see why there have to be so many religions and so many different types of philosophical speculation about how our world came into being and what we as humans mean in relation to it.

Comment — The traditions of antiquity confirm that at one time in the early history of mankind there was One Wisdom known to all the nations of earth, but gradually so many false interpretations of this or that aspect of truth gained supremacy that it was deemed necessary for Saviors or Avatāras periodically to "incarnate" among men in order to restore the ancient values. They did not come to found a new religion; their followers did that, with a zeal not always matched by fidelity to the spirit of the message. It is the same sad story of human nature seeking to preserve the *words* of truth by getting them so neatly inscribed into a book or manuscript that once this occurs there is nothing left to do but to store it away carefully! All too soon, not only have we "lost" the key to it, but we have forgotten its original high purpose. Before we know it, we are taking someone else's say-so as our authority for what is true or not true! Truth is one, but there are as many "truths" or expressions of "divine things" as there are human beings to reflect their insight through the prism of their own individual consciousness.

More About Theosophy

BEFORE WE DISCUSS the "modern school" of theosophy — by which is meant the several organizations that have sprung up since 1875 — I should like to lay some further ground-work of thought.

As we look into the history and development of the various religious philosophies of the past, it is interesting to note a common pattern. A Messenger appears — a Christ or a Buddha, a Zoroaster or Krishna — and is welcomed by the few, while his message either goes unnoticed or is denounced as false and dangerous to the *status quo*. He leaves, and his disciples of that day or of succeeding generations, waking at last to some recognition of his teaching, start to build an organization — the holy words are written down, centers of worship established, sacraments are used as a means of salvation, and the once *living* message becomes a creed. Future believers, guided mainly by the outer forms, soon disagree among themselves, and in no long time the original nucleus of the 'new revelation' splits into fragments.

Typical of human nature, we find on the one hand the ultra-conservatives who cling rigidly to the letter of doctrine, insisting that their interpretation is the one and final authority. On the other hand, and diametrically opposed, are the ultra-liberalists who in their zeal to overthrow every restriction lose all sense of proportion, confuse their values and often end by seeing black as white and wrong as right. Between the two extremes are those who steadfastly try to follow the 'middle way' in their effort to interpret the message and to rediscover, behind the formal and the traditional, the divine motif.

This is nothing strange, for it is manifest in every phase of human experience: in business, in education, in social conduct as well as in national and international affairs. And so it has been with theosophy in its earlier forms, just as it is today with regard to its modern expressions where the lines of divergence have by now become fairly marked. We are speaking here of *qualities* which cut across all man-made barriers, for in every organization may be found, in varying degree, all three types of adherents. Hopefully there will always be a sufficient number, whether attached to one or another organization or to none, who will endeavor to keep alive a knowledge of the original *theosophia* or god-wisdom — not by seeking to escape life's hard responsibilities, but by an intelligent and practical application of its philosophy to the growing needs of men.

Question — But how is one to know what is genuine and what is not? I have done considerable reading in all sorts of books. Some of the ideas seem like old friends, even though they're new to me, but I found other things I didn't like at all.

Comment — Unfortunately, there are various interpretations of theosophy being promulgated these days, and it is not a simple matter to discern what is true and what is false. If one is seriously interested in digging out the pure doctrine that inspired the founder of the modern school, he should go directly to the source and familiarize himself with its principles. In this way he will have a basis by which to test any later interpretations.

Question — You say the "pure doctrine" — does that mean theosophy has specific tenets which one must believe? Or can one pick and choose what he likes, and leave the rest?

Comment — In all her writings, H. P. Blavatsky makes it clear that theosophy has absolutely no creed or formula of belief, no set of dogmas to which one must adhere, each individual being entirely free to select what appeals to him. If we are rooted in the same Divine Intelligence that produced the cosmos, we not only have the privilege but are expected to grow and develop in accordance with our *own* character, not another's. Under no circumstances should we feel bound by the intellectual or moral or even spiritual pressures of anything but our own inner 'sense.' Whatever we read or hear, in any field of thought, should always pass the test of our own highest judgment. If it rings true to us, we should accept it, for the time being at least, until we see a larger facet of truth. If it does not, we can just cast it aside. We may be rejecting something which later on will prove of essential worth; but if at the moment it does not seem right, either we are not ready for it, or that particular truth will, perhaps, do us more lasting good in the future.

Question — But there must be some definite teachings which belong to theosophy, aren't there? Or is it mainly a kind of philanthropic effort, such as working for better conditions, and that sort of thing?

Comment — No, genuine theosophy is not simply a vague brand of do-good psychology, without relation to man and his pressing need to know who he is and what is his ultimate role on earth. Nevertheless, because an underlying 'love of mankind' motivated its re-presentation, it is clearly a 'philanthropic' effort — using the word in its pure sense.

Is it then a religion, or perhaps a new kind of philosophy? Actually it is neither and both; in fact, theosophy has been called the mother of all religions and philosophies.

Question — Wouldn't that explain why we find so many points of similarity in the great religions? I remember how struck I was by this when I took a course in comparative religion. At the time I hadn't traveled much and knew very little about other peoples, but the professor we had was a profound student of the *Upanishads* as well as of the ancient Greek and Roman writings, and more than once he referred to a "golden thread" of wisdom which, he said, could lead us through the maze of the many interpretations.

Comment — There is indeed a "golden thread" of truth, connecting the most archaic forms of belief with the present, and linking the spiritual traditions of every nation and race to that spark of Divine Intelligence that is at the core of every man.

Question — I think I'm getting beyond my depth. I'd like to refer again to Webster, and get these various ideas related to what he said.

Comment — Of course. Part 1 of the definition, you may recall, pertains to theosophy with a small *t*, as it found outlet in varying ways in preceding centuries. If we paraphrase it now in simpler terms, we can see how universally applicable it is to *every* religious or philosophic system that has at its heart the theme of Deity as the fountainhead and origin of all beings and things:

theosophia, or knowledge concerning the movements and work-habits of Divinity as it seeks to imbody itself in a universe (and in every portion thereof, inclusive of human beings), such knowledge being achieved either by direct spiritual insight or by study or philosophic reflection, or by a fruitful blend of the mind with the intuition.

Question — I can't imagine any of us reaching that stage of enlightenment in one life. Maybe that is why reincarnation was so popular among many peoples, because they felt it would take more than one life to make the grade.

Comment — None of us is expected to make the grade to this extent in a single lifetime! That would be as absurd as to expect the first-grader immediately to pass the entrance examinations of a university. Nevertheless, as St. John reminded us, within every man *is* "the Light," and one day we will have earned our own vision of "divine things." In the meantime, we can take courage, for even within the relatively short period of recorded history there have been those great and noble souls who were sufficiently advanced over the rest of us to dare the heights. They had traveled, perhaps for many, many lifetimes, the lonely path of self-discipline, self-mastery and self-illumination — to suffer, at last, the crucifixion of their earthly nature that the god within might take fuller birth within their souls. Such have been the leaders and guides of mankind, the long line of Saviors and Christs who, on the consummation of their sacred experience, have shared of their "vision" with others, and in so doing have wrought vast changes in the spiritual and psychological destiny of the peoples among whom they lived.

They did not come to reveal a new set of truths, or even to found a new religion. As H. P. Blavatsky says, all of them were *"transmitters,* not original thinkers. They were the authors of new forms and interpretations, while the truths upon which the latter were based were as old as mankind."

Question — That makes sense to me. And if my logic is sound, all of them would naturally teach the same thing. If they really had experienced their 'moment of truth,' wouldn't they have contacted the identic divine source?

Comment — Precisely, and that is why when we look into the world religions and the various mystical and philosophic systems we discover that all of them, when pared to their essentials, tell the same story. We sometimes forget that our knowledge of our past racial history is scant, based on a mere five or six thousand years, whereas the traditions of many ancient peoples go back hundreds of millennia — every one of them pointing to an archaic wisdom-religion as the perennial fount of Truth from which all human knowledge has been drawn. So old, its origins cannot be traced, yet its existence is confirmed by the periodic incarnation of Men whose towering spiritual stature made them the inspired leaders of progressive civilizations.

Question — But this wisdom-religion surely wasn't called theosophy way back there, was it?

Comment — No, indeed. Names are completely incidental, for truth takes any and every name, depending upon a number of causes. Different peoples in different cycles call for different types of guidance. At one time we find emphasis on the devotional or religious aspect, as in early Christianity, with the urgent call to strive for 'Christ-consciousness' or 'mystical union' with the Father within. At another, the philosophic basis of man's many-faceted nature comes in for study, as in Plato's day, or in ancient India and Egypt and among other peoples of the time. Then again, we have eras when science takes the forefront in extensive investigation of natural law. But always, whether it is universally venerated or for a period goes underground, *truth is the inheritance of all who qualify.*

One more point, if I may, before we take up part 2 of our definition. A few moments ago someone wondered if theosophy included any system of doctrines. If we turn to *The Secret Doctrine* we will see that it does indeed embrace a systematic exposition of philosophic principles — themselves derived from the wisdom-teaching of antiquity — which principles describe the "birth of worlds and of man" through many rounds of experience. But, as the author repeatedly says, she herself was only a transmitter; she brought nothing

225

new, her task being to cast the searchlight of interest on this treasury of "wisdom" concealed beneath the tangle of mystical and religious lore of past civilizations.

Question — Is this the reason she formed the Theosophical Society, or did she have other goals in mind?

Question — I understood she tried to establish a brotherhood among the various races, but I guess the times were against this.

Comment — In matters of the spirit, we cannot measure success or failure by ordinary standards. Despite the constant threat of global war, the *idea* of brotherhood has taken hold of the consciousness of peoples everywhere, which in itself is a tremendous advance. While the underlying purpose of the parent society was the sharing of this ancient knowledge concerning the structure and operations of nature, physical and divine, its chief objective was to coalesce into a nucleus those men and women who were dedicated to the accomplishment of the ideal you mention. And as true brotherhood must be *universal* — without regard to superficial differences of color, race or creed — this could not, of course, be achieved without some bridges of understanding being built among the great variety of peoples in every continent. Therefore, an unbiased study of all religions, philosophies and sciences, ancient and modern, was encouraged, along with an investigation of the inner constitution of man and his relation to the areas of consciousness, higher and lower, in which he participates.

This is a very broad program and, human nature being what it is, the original objectives have not been attained. Nevertheless, a torch was once more held aloft. It may take centuries before an enlightened fraternity of nations is a reality, yet progress is evident in the growing awareness that not only are all men brothers, but that every religious truth (not dogma) draws its sustenance from one imperishable source.

Now then, let us take a careful look at Webster's second definition. In the first place it is misleading, in that modern theosophy as expounded by H. P. Blavatsky was not intended exclusively to follow "Buddhistic and Brahmanic theories." Even a cursory review of her writings shows that she utilized the traditions and scriptures of *all* countries in order to illustrate their origin in the One Perennial Wisdom. The sagas and mythology of the Scandinavian *Eddas*, the Jewish theosophy of the Kabbālāh, the teachings and discipline of Pythagoras and Plato, of Ammonius Saccas and the Neoplatonists, as well as the writings of Lao-tzŭ and Confucius of China, are all discussed along with Christianity, Buddhism and the philosophy of the *Upanishads* and the *Bhagavad-Gītā*.

Question — How do you account for the use of so many Oriental terms in her books? It seems to me these ideas could have been put in simpler language. Yet even as I say this, I begin to ask myself, for instance, what English word I would use instead of karma!

Comment — That's the point. Some later writers have perhaps gone too far in the use of unfamiliar terminology, which may be advisable if one is writing a technical exposition; but for introductory literature it doesn't seem necessary. There are cases when the use of technical language is essential; science, for example, in all its branches, uses hundreds of technical terms which give to its specialists information at a glance, but which to the layman mean very little.

You mentioned karma. It so happens that when H. P. Blavatsky was writing her books (and the situation holds even today), there wasn't any word in English, or in any of our modern European tongues, able to convey what this one Sanskrit term implies. So when the word karma with its philosophical implications was introduced to the West, it became so indispensable that it was soon adopted into our language, in the same way as have thousands of other foreign terms. Now we could say that karma means just what St. Paul did when he wrote to the Galatians that God is not mocked and that as a man sows he will reap. But look how many words we have used when the one word karma, if properly understood, conveys all that and more.

Question — I can see how some of these terms are very helpful. But what does Webster mean by saying that modern theosophy teaches a kind of "pantheistic evolution"?

Question — When you speak of a person as a pantheist, doesn't that mean he worships many gods rather than believing in one Supreme Being?

Comment — That is one interpretation, but a secondary one only, which doesn't actually convey what the term signifies. Unfortunately we in the West have a habit of looking down our noses at any concept that does not immediately dovetail with our own ideas. The word itself is also from the Greek — *pan* + *theos*, or "all divine" — and originally meant that all has sprung forth from Deity. For so many centuries, however, we have placed God outside and apart from ourselves, that any belief that suggests Divinity as the source of all beings and things is said to "smack of pantheism." Hence it is regarded with disfavor because it is wrongly understood to mean that everything *is* God — and what blasphemy to say that a stone or a horse, or even a human being is God!

But if by the phrase "pantheistic evolution" we conceive an evolution based on the premise that every point in space — which comprises every inhabitant from atom to star in our solar system and in the myriads of solar systems that make up the Milky Way and beyond — is an expression of Deity because housing an *aspect* of it, then, as I understand it, theosophy all through the centuries has endorsed this type of "pantheism." And this would naturally include the corollary idea that all such living beings, no matter what their evolutionary status, are constantly renewing themselves — using one vehicle or body after another in order that the god-spark within, which animates its series of vehicles, may grow and evolve and gain enrichment through this experience. With the human kingdom, the method of this cyclic return is called reincarnation, which means that the human soul enters and informs a human body.

Question — I'm so glad to hear you say this because the subject of reincarnation is the main thing that appealed to me in the books I've read. It may be because it has been a conviction with me since childhood when a very dear friend of my father, a minister by the way, told me about it. I was seven or eight, and one Sunday after dinner he took me for a walk along the river. It was autumn and the trees were all flame and gold. He said he wanted me to remember always how beautiful they were just before they would seem to die; only that they didn't really die, but just lost their leaves for a while so they could rest and grow fresh ones in the spring. Perhaps he might not have made so deep an impression except that a few weeks later he died suddenly. For a while I was heartbroken, and then his words came to me as a wonderful comfort, and ever since I have felt a growing certainty that death cannot put an end to love and sympathy and all those intangibles that are so real a part of human life.

Comment — I have long felt that if this one doctrine of the soul's rebirth were restored to Christian teaching where it was once included, it would exert a powerful influence on Western psychology and by so much on world relationships. If reincarnation were linked in a positive way with its companion teaching of karma, men and women everywhere would realize they were gods in essence, whose future destiny was theirs to make and therefore bright with promise, as nothing would be impossible of attainment.

It could be that in this twentieth century these archaic truths will have another opportunity to override the literalists as well as the fantasy-mongers. It may be called the esoteric philosophy of the past, but it will be more than that. It will be divinity's inspiration to man when he first became man, which inspiration is still lying dormant in the breast of every human being. That is what the Master Jesus referred to when he said: "Before Abraham was, I am"; and what the Psalmist had in mind when he sang: "Yea, though I walk through the valley of the shadow of death . . . Thou art with me."

Man Will Survive

A LETTER FROM A FRIEND expresses the feeling that there seems to him some deeper purpose unfolding, some undefined but clearly felt challenge, as though not only individuals here and there, but humanity in general were being called upon to do and to *be* above and beyond anything we have so far achieved. He said that among his business associates he had noted an increasing rebellion against the old type of hard materialism and a definite, though perhaps unrecognized, reaching out toward something beyond what they had so far understood. But, he added, in spite of a current of optimism among many that decency and right will in the

231

end win out, there is a great deal of fear and bewilderment, and people are wondering how to prepare for what they feel may be developing.

It is certainly not given us to know precisely what is ahead; in fact, it would be a hazardous situation for any of us to be able to see the future in detail. The protective reason is obvious, for the moment one believes he knows exactly what is going to happen, he begins, unconsciously, to prepare for it — *outwardly* or objectively; and in so doing he may completely unprepare himself for it — *inwardly*. He invariably creates imaginary possibilities which become unnecessary roadblocks against the natural intuitive guidance that would otherwise have been his to help him handle each event as it comes, and not before.

How then can we prepare for the future? We cannot prepare for this or that event, because we don't know what will occur tomorrow or the next day or a year from now. But if we can establish our lives upon the solid foundation of principle — whatever our religious or philosophic views — and try to live the *essence* of our spiritual heritage, it will not matter what type of experience we or the nations of the world must meet. Our consciousness will automatically respond with the exact quality of thought and deed required for whatever eventuality the future may hold.

Moreover, all through the cycles of human growth, in every country and in every age, there have been and are today unknown and unpublicized individuals who bring to bear their quiet yet potent influence upon the destinies of their respective nations. They do not labor in the hope of recognition or personal gain, but solely that justice and freedom will eventually prevail. We rarely, if ever, hear of them; and there may be among them those who are quite unaware of the extent or depth of their task, whom they are serving, and to what good ends. But is not this one of the ways in which the Guardians of humanity find, accept and train new "laborers in the field"?

Those great souls who have the responsibility for the enlightenment of man and his protection into the future are surely as active today with their assistance as they ever were. If we could catch sufficient of their vision to glimpse even a little of the inner purport of their work, we would know that it encompasses every avenue of experience. And while we cannot discern the specific activities of these silent benefactors, we can feel their impact on world thought. Books and periodicals, even the daily press, show an increasing trend toward a freer and clearer expression of those innate Ideas which are the fountain and source of the world's treasury of wisdom. Now, once again, these ideas are coming into their own; but not without a struggle, for the stronger the urge toward liberation, the harder do the opposing forces work. Yet the very intensity of the opposition by those who would keep the human spirit in chains, grooved to a prescribed mode of thought and aspiration, attests to the growing strength of those who labor for the progress of the race. In the crucible of man's consciousness a powerful alchemy is taking place, while the prophecy of nearly a century ago is being enacted before our eyes:

Plato was right: *ideas* rule the world; and, as men's minds will receive *new* ideas, laying aside the old and effete, the world will advance: mighty revolutions will spring from them; creeds and even powers will crumble before their onward march crushed by the irresistible force. It will be just as impossible to resist their influx, when the time comes, as to stay the progress of the tide. But all this will come gradually on, and before it comes we have a duty set before us; that of sweeping away as much as possible the dross left to us by our pious forefathers. New ideas have to be planted on clean places, for these ideas touch upon the most momentous subjects.

It is not physical phenomena but these universal ideas that we study, as to comprehend the former, we have to first understand the latter. They touch man's true position in the universe, in relation to his previous and future births; his origin and ultimate destiny; the relation of the mortal to the immortal; of the temporary to the eternal; of the finite to the infinite; ideas larger, grander, more comprehensive, recognizing the universal reign of Immutable Law, unchanging and unchangeable in regard to which there is only an ETERNAL Now, while to uninitiated mortals time is past or future as related to their finite existence on this material speck of dirt.   — K.H.*

And undergirding all is the earnest hope that one day a true "Universal Fraternity" will embrace the whole of mankind.

Those of us who profess to have a sincere desire to add our mite to the betterment of man should ask ourselves: are we interested solely in the light which these great ideas can shed on our own limited environment, or are we moved to live and work so that the sun of truth may shine in the souls of all men everywhere?

Many people today are thinking along these broad and unconfined lines — clergymen and scientists, educators and writers, businessmen and housewives — trying to link together the scattered hints which for centuries have been covered by the dust of literalism. Few of us may understand "man's true position in the universe" or our relation to "previous and future births"; but all of us will respond to the truth of our origin in Divinity and to the challenge of our

*From the collection of Mahatma letters, housed in the Department of Select Manuscripts of the British Museum.

ultimate triumph over the weight of material existence, as the strength of our spirit takes permanent hold. If but a handful of men and women, in any part of the globe and of any or no faith, could fully liberate themselves from the enslaving influence of "the old and effete," there is no foreseeing what extraordinary effect this would have on the generations to come.

The emancipating force of these cosmic ideas is gathering momentum. When and where it will reach its crest, no one can say. But if my guess is correct, its expression will exceed anything that has occurred in the history of civilization. It will not be proclaimed with words or the blaring of trumpets; the language of the soul needs no words or noisy symbol. But we can be certain that if the inner call of humanity continues to increase in volume, an entirely new concept of life will find manifestation in high places and low.

All of this sounds fine, you say, but how will it help us to meet our problems here and now? We might not feel so bewildered if we could realize that man is not an isolated species, but is part of a cosmic pattern of growth in which the whole universe is involved. When our astronomers tell us that our own solar system is but one of trillions in space and, among the countless billions of planetary systems whirling around their individual central suns, that innumerable ones may well be 'life-bearing,' they are reaching to the very core of the mystery of growth. It means that the inhabitants of those stars and planets must also, like us humans, be gods in their inmost, housing themselves in temples of matter!

If we could observe the flow of history from the earliest beginnings of the evolution of a universe, which includes man's origin as well as all the kingdoms above and below him, we would see the vivifying of manifold forms by Divinity and the simultaneous awakening of the material aspect of nature, as the spark of life seeks vehicle after vehicle in which to imbody itself. Simply phrased, Spirit impregnates Matter by involving itself in increasing degree in bodies until it reaches the densest point of its cycle; the pendulum then swings upward and Spirit again emerges, causing the material to lose its dominance.

That of course is a very broad picture, but it is significant that in every ancient tradition the same "idea" is found. There must be a practical reason for this, because the more we brood upon the philosophy behind it, the greater bearing does it seem to have on our own personal development.

Let us, for the moment, think of ourselves not as human beings but as divinities — god-sparks — progressing since the very dawn of 'creation' along our vast pilgrimage through material existence until we arrived at that crucial point when Man, as we know him today, had to be born. True, we were compounded of Spirit and Matter, of divine spark and body. But there was as yet no awareness of ourselves. Here we find Spirit in a unique manner fusing with Matter to bring forth a third element: the fire of Mind. From child-humans merely existing in a Garden of Eden we became self-conscious 'living souls,' knowing good from evil and recognizing innately that henceforth we would have to endure the hardship of self-imposed discipline as we earned our way toward godhood. This is where we stand today: product of spirit and matter we are indeed gods in essence, but as far as our present evolution goes, we are still in our *human* phase!

We can see then that these truths, which were given to us at the beginning of our present racial cycle, are as sound and as strengthening as they ever were and will remain valid until we graduate to a higher level of growth. That being the case, it behooves us to learn what those truths are and how to adapt them in our lives. They are the basis of the ancient philosophies of India, Greece and Persia, Egypt and China, of the Norse and Germanic traditions, and of the ancient Americas, and certainly form the heart and core of the teaching of the Master Jesus. Once we experience their practical spiritual worth, we won't need to know with our brains what is around the next bend. We shall be prepared inwardly to meet any exigency.

The world is moving so tempestuously, and psychologies and mental concepts are changing with such rapidity that it is difficult to keep one's equilibrium. But that is precisely what we must do. And if the times are demanding that humanity as a whole take another step forward and *be* above and beyond what we have ever been, why should you and I exempt ourselves? No one of us is separate and apart from the karma of the race. We are part and parcel of the struggling human life-wave, and as we weather our own personality storms and meet with courage our individual heartaches and trials, so will we affect for good the thought climate of the world.

The paradox is that the very impact of global tensions is providing us with the exact stage setting essential to progress — the opportunity to develop a deeper quality of spiritual self-reliance. Hence there must be no intermediary between a man's will to grow and the god-spark within. No priest, no friend, no ideal even, however noble, must come between us and our God, for anything we cling to selfishly will block off the natural guidance from within. All we can do is to try to live to the full capacity of our understanding those universal spiritual principles which have stood the test of time, but we dare not tell another how to apply that garnered wisdom to his own life. For who are we to say that *our* concept of what is good and unselfish is right for anyone else? He alone must judge that. This is why growth is primarily an individual affair — an everliving progression of the soul as it moves from the less to the greater, from the self-centered to the selfless, from the darkness to the light.

No one of us may look backwards or sideways or in any direction other than forwards. If we allow our attention and our interest to be deflected, even for the briefest interval, from the direct path that our immortal self has indicated for us — which amounts in simple terms to adhering to that which we inwardly sense to be honest and true and for the benefit of all rather than only for ourselves — we run the risk of having our ideals, our devotion, even our love for the highest we would serve, turn to salt. As the Master Jesus expressed it to his disciples: "Remember Lot's wife. Whosoever shall seek to save his life shall lose it; and whosoever shall lose his life shall preserve it."

The present confusion of ideals has brought us to a dangerous pass — and I am not referring to the perils from missiles and rockets, satellites or bombs. Those are symptoms, and alarming ones in the hands of the willfully destructive; but they are symptoms only and do not constitute *Man.* Should the much-feared destruction of civilization eventuate — which I very much doubt will occur — we will have to rely on the simple yet all-inclusive truth that you may destroy the body but you cannot kill life. *Man will survive;* he will face and surmount every cataclysm that may be in store, whether by flood, fire, outer space — or himself!

Nations and races, as such, have time and again passed out of existence, but the egos that once inhabited them incarnate anew, in other lands and in other racial strains. If we can grasp that larger vision as far as is humanly possible, this will not remove the dangers, but it will help us to meet whatever comes with fortitude.

So let us take courage and join hands with those clear-sighted and strong individuals in every country who are quietly working to keep the wheels of progress moving forward.

INDEX

241